INTERNATIONAL BLACK SEA UNIVERSITY
FACULTY OF EDUCATION AND HUMANITIES
M.A. PROGRAM IN ENGLISH PHILOLOGY

THE CASE FOR SPELLING REFORMS IN ENGLISH

Carl Reinhold Augustsson

Master's Thesis in English Philology

Tbilisi, 2019

Scientific Supervisor: Prof. Dr. Zaal Kikvidze

(full name & academic title)

I confirm that the work corresponds to the field, is characterized by novelty, scientific and practical value and is presented by the format defined by International Black Sea University.

(supervisor's signature)

Reviewers (full name & academic title):

Dr. Lia Todua

I acknowledge that this is my own work, which is presented in the format defined by International Black Sea University.

(master's student's signature)

Table of Contents

ACKNOWLEDGEMENTS i

DEDICATION ii

ABSTRACT iii

რეზიუმე vi

INTRODUCTION ix

CHAPTER 1. LITERATURE ON SPELLING REFORM AND HISTORICAL OVERVIEW 1

CHAPTER 2. SPELLING REFORMS IN OTHER LANGUAGES 15

CHAPTER 3. THE PRACTICALITIES OF SPELLING REFORM 37

CHAPTER 4. SUGGESTED NEW WAY OF SPELLING THE ENGLISH LANGUAGE 52

CONCLUSIONS 90

REFERENCES   95

APPENDIX 1: John- Chapter 3 (Holy Bible, New
International Version) in the Current Orthography   100

APPENDIX 2: John -Chapter 3 (Holy Bible, New
International Version) in the Reformed Orthography with
Diacritics   104

APPENDIX 3: John -Chapter 3 (Holy Bible, New
International Version) in the Reformed Orthography without
Diacritics   107

ABOUT THE AUTHOR   111

ACKNOWLEDGEMENTS

I would like to acknowledge my supervisor, Zaal Kikvidze, my reviewer, Lia Todua, and my department head, Nikoloz Parjanadze, all of whom made this program quite enjoyable.

DEDICATION

I would like to dedicate this work to my wife Manana (მანანა) and our children, Anna (ანნა) and Alexander (ალექსანდერ), whose loving support and understanding helped me to finish this work.

Also, I wanted to dedicate this to everyone, both native English-speaking children and speakers of foreign languages, who are learning English, and who therefore have to deal with an orthographic system that is ridiculously complicated and should have been overhauled centuries ago.

ABSTRACT

English is probably the least phonetically spelled language (amongst those written with an alphabet) anywhere on the planet. If alphabets are supposed to accurately indicate the manner in which words are to be pronounced, then there is no question that the current spelling of English is a huge failure. If the manner in which English words are spoken has changed, then should not the manner in which the words are written change as well? The purpose of this research is to examine how English spelling can be made more phonetic.

The first chapter gives all of the relevant background information. The first thing it includes is a literature review. After that, the rest of the chapter focuses on the history of the English language. In order to understand how this situation came into being, it is necessary to know the history of the English language. This subchapter is divided into three sections. The first one is about the history of the English language in general. In this section, the unique history of English—that it is actually a combination of several other European languages—is explored. In the second one, the history of English pronunciation and orthography is discussed. One of the reasons why English is so unphonetic is that a great vowel shift occurred in the High Middle Ages, with little change in orthography. The final section deals with the previous—and obviously, unsuccessful—attempts at spelling reform.

The second chapter is about spelling reforms in other languages. After all, in order to reform English spelling, it helps to see how the same process occurred in other languages. There are two ways in which spelling can be reformed: a change in the current system, or a change from one system to another. The first half of the chapter deals with languages that underwent a change from one writing system to another. The most famous example of this is Turkish, which went from being written in the Arabic abjad to the Latin alphabet. Also discussed in this subchapter are the reasons why certain countries choose certain writing systems. Religion is often the biggest reason. The second subchapter explores spelling reforms in which the same writing system—usually an alphabet—is kept, but reformed. A number of examples are mentioned. Some of these examples, such as Russian and Greek, do not include the Latin alphabet, whereas others, such as French and German, do. Many of the other languages of Western European origin have undergone some type of spelling reform in the past thirty years.

Chapter three, the shortest chapter, discusses the practical issues surrounding any attempt to reform English Orthography. Also mentioned in this chapter are the positives and negatives of spelling reform. The biggest positive is obvious: it will be much easier to spell English words, which will make it easier for both native-speaking children and foreigners learning how to write English. The negatives include issues such as the fact that so many books have already been printed and that people will have to learn a new system.

Chapter four is the actual proposed reform itself. The first issue explored is whether diacritics should be used. After that, first the consonant and then the vowel sounds are studied one by one. Finally, a new orthography is suggested.

The conclusion ends with a sentence in the suggested new English orthography:

Let's fīnulē cāj ðu wā wē spel Iŋliš wurdz sō ðat it wil bē mor funetik!

რეზიუმე

მთელს მსოფლიოში ინგლისური ენის ორთოგრავია შესაძლოა (იმ ენათა შორის, რომლებიც ანბანით იწერება) ყველაზე ნაკლებ ადეკვატურია მისი ფონეტიკისა. თუ ანბანი უნდა მიგვანიშნებდეს სიტყვების სწორად წარმოთქმაზე, მაშინ ინგლისური ენის ამჟამინდელი მართლწერა უდაო კრახს წარმოადგენს. დროთა განმავლობაში ინგლისურში სიტყვების წარმოთქმის წესი იცვლება, მაშასადამე, მათი წერის წესიც ხომ უნდა შეიცვალოს? ამ კვლევის მიზანია შეისწავლოს, თუ როგორ შეიძლება ინგლისური უფრო ფონეტიკურად და მარტივად საწერი გავხადოთ.

პირველი თავი გვაწვდის ძირითად ინფორმაციას კვლევის შესახებ. უპირველესად იგი შეიცავს ლიტერატურის მიმოხილვას. ამის შემდეგ ფოკუსი გადადის ინგლისური ენის ისტორიაზე, რისი ცოდნაც აუცილებელია, რათა გავერკვიოთ დღევანდელი ინგლისური მართლწერის პრობლემებში. ეს ქვეთავი დაყოფილია სამ ნაწილად. პირველი ნაწილია ინგლისური ენის საერთო ისტორია, სადაც ნაჩვენებია ის საკითხი, რომ ინგლისური ენა წარმოადგენს რამოდენიმე ევროპული ენის ნაზავს. მეორე ნაწილში წარმოთქმისა და ორთოგრაფიის ისტორიაა განხილული. ერთ-ერთი მიზეზი რამაც გამოიწვია ინგლისურის ასეთი არაფონეტიკურობა არის ის, რომ ხმოვანთა წარმოთქმის წესები შუა საუკუნეებში შეიცვალა. ბოლო ნაწილში კი

განხილულია წინა და აშკარად წარუმატებელი რაფორმები, რომლითაც სცადეს ინგლისური მართლწერის შეცვლა.

მეორე თავში ნაჩვენებია სხვა ენებში განხორციელებული მართლწერის რეფორმები. იმისათვის რომ ინგლისურში განვახორციელოთ ცვლილებები უნდა ვნახოთ ეს პროცესი როგორ ჩატარდა სხვა ენებში. არსებობს მართლწერის შეცვლის ორი გზა: შეიცვალოს ამჟამინდელი სისტემა ან ერთი სისტემიდან მეორეზე გადასვლა განხორციელდეს. თავის პირველ ნაწილში განხილულია ენები რომლებიც ერთი დამწერლობიდან მეორეზე გადავიდნენ. ამის ყველაზე ნათელი მაგალითია თურქული ენა, რომელიც არაბული დამწერლობიდან ლათინურ ანბანზე გადავიდა. ასევე ამ ქვეთავში განხილულია საკითხი იმისა, გარკვეული ქვეყნები რატომ ირჩევენ ამა თუ იმ დამწერლობას. რელიგია ხშირად ამის ერთ-ერთი უდიდესი მიზეზია. მეორე ქვეთავში გამოკვლეულია ის შემთხვევები, როდესაც იგივე დამწერლობა დატოვეს, მაგრამ მართლწერა შეცვალა. რამოდენიმე მაგალითია მოყვანილი, ისეთები როგორიცაა რუსული და ბერძნული, ასევე ლათინური დამწერლობის ენები ფრანგული და გერმანული. ბევრმა სხვა დასავლეთ ევროპულმა ენამაც განიცადა მართლწერის ცვლილება ბოლო ოცდაათი წლის განმავლობაში.

მესამე ნაწილი, ყველაზე მოკლე, განიხილავს პრაქტიკულ საკითხებს დაკავშირებულს ინგლისური ორთოგრაფიის რეფორმის მცდელობისთან. აქვეა ნახსენები მართლწერის რეფორმის დადებითი და უარყოფითი მხარეები. ყველაზე დიდი დადებითი მხარე ნათელია: გაცილებით ადვილი გახდება ინგლისურ ენაზე წერა. ეს საგრძნობლად გაამარტივებს ინგლისურის წერას როგორც ადგილობრივი მოლაპარაკეებისთვის, ასევე უცხოელებისთვის, ვისაც ინგლისურს სწავლა სურთ. ადგილობრივი მოსაუბრეთა პრობლემა ისიც იქნება, რომ უამრავი წიგნია უკვე დაწერილი და ხალხს ახალი სისტემის სწავლა მოუწევს.

მეოთხე თავი თავად შემოთავაზებულ რეფორმას წარმოადგენს. აქ განხილულია დიაგიტი ნიშნების ხმარების საჭიროება და შემდეგ ჯერ თანხოვნები და შემდგომ ხმოვნები ცალ-ცალკე არის შესწავლილი. და დასკვნისთვის გთავაზობთ ახალ ორთოგრაფიას.

ნაშრომი მთავრდება წინადადებით, რომელიც ახალი, შემოთავაზებული ინგლისური ორთოგრაფიითაა დაწერილი

Let's fīnulē cāj ðu wā wē spel Iŋliš wurdz sō ðat it wil bē mor funetik!

INTRODUCTION

Why is it that the words "bomb", "comb", and "tomb" don't rhyme, whereas the words "rude", "food", and "lewd" do (Indeed, even the word "do" somewhat rhymes with the previous three)? Indeed, *The Washington Post* mentions this. "When "say," "they" and "weigh" rhyme, but "bomb," "comb" and "tomb" don't, wuudn't it maek mor sens to spel wurdz the wae thae sound?" (Superville, 2006) Based on the spellings of the words, the exact opposite should be true. There are plenty of other examples of this, such as the fact that "few" and "sew" sound nothing like each other. Indeed. "sew" does not even sound like "sewer". The classic example of a letter combination making different sounds is "ough", as it makes a different sound in the words "thought", "though", "through", and "tough". Likewise, the letter "c" appears three times in "Pacific Ocean", but spells a different sound each time.

An even better example is the simple "ea" vowel combination. Take this sentence: I hear that you learned to create, break, and eat heart-shaped bread while watching reality television. The "ea" combination appears eight different times in this sentence. Yet, it makes a different sound in all eight cases. By the way, it is important to note that all eight of these words are common words of English origin and are therefore not based on a foreign system of orthography.

This same phenomenon manifests itself in other ways. For example, the written word "minute" has two different pronunciations, referring to two different spoken words that mean two different things. Indeed, the two different spoken words are not even the same part of speech.

The flipside is also true in that the words "no" and "know" have the exact same pronunciation.

Another example, the difference in pronunciation between "lose" and "loose" is the difference between an "s" and "z" sound, yet the spelling difference is between one "o" and two, even though both words have the exact same vowel sound. Likewise, the difference in pronunciation between "desert" and "dessert" is the difference between stress on the first syllable versus stress on the second, yet the spelling difference is one "s" versus two, even though both words have the exact same "s" sound.

What this small handful—and there are so many more within the English language—shows is that English is probably the worst spelled language ever, and certainly amongst European languages written with the Latin alphabet. The reasons for this will be explored in the coming chapters. However, what this clearly shows is that spelling reform in English is long overdue. After all, the purpose of an alphabet-based writing system (along with certain other writing systems such as abjads and syllabaries) is to indicate the manner in which the word is to be pronounced. If that is the case, then the status quo in English is an utter failure.

The purpose of this research is to examine the feasibility of reforming the spelling system in English and to propose an updated, far more phonetic way of spelling the English language.

In order to do this, it will be necessary to examine several important issues related to this topic. First of all, it will be necessary to look at a brief history of the English language and how we ended up in this situation where English spelling is highly unphonetic. This study of the history of the

English language will include a brief look at earlier calls for spelling reform, of which there have been at least several noteworthy ones.

Next, it will be useful to look at spelling reforms in other languages to see how a similar reform would work in English. There are two different ways that spelling reforms have occurred in other languages. The first type is a change in the writing system. A good example of this is when Turkey changed from using the Arabic abjad to the Latin alphabet for writing the Turkish language. This discussion will also include a review as to why different societies choose the writing systems that they do. The second type of spelling reform in other languages is a reform of the manner in which a language is written using the same writing system, usually an alphabet.

After researching such background information, the next step will be to study the feasibility of spelling reform in English. While discussing the feasibility of such a reform, the pros and cons will also be mentioned.

After all of that, it will finally be possible to suggest a better way to spell the English language. The first step in order to do that is to decide which diacritics, if any, should be used. In order to do that, a review of the diacritics that are available in the Latin alphabet and how they are used in other languages, especially fellow European languages, will be necessary. In the same vein, letters that used to exist in English will be mentioned, along with deciding whether some or all of them should be brought back.

CHAPTER 1. LITERATURE ON SPELLING REFORM AND HISTORICAL OVERVIEW

Introduction to Chapter 1

The best way to begin is with relevant background information. This chapter will focus first on the literature review. The second half of the chapter will be about the history of the English language itself. The second half of this chapter itself will be sub-divided into several sections. The first section will be a brief overview of the history of English pronunciation and orthography. The second section will explore previous—and mostly unsuccessful—attempts at spelling reform in English. Prior to these two sections though, there will be a review of the history of the English language in general, and not just about the pronunciation and orthography. Background information with regards to orthography and spelling reform in other languages—which will also prove quite helpful to this study—will not be in this chapter. Instead, this background information will be in the second chapter.

1.1. Literature Search Strategy

A variety of sources were used to research this topic. These sources included books, journal articles, newspapers (mainly online versions), and websites. Different types of sources were more helpful for different parts of the research. In order to best review the literature, it is best to mention the different types of literature used on a chapter by chapter basis.

The websites of Omniglot and Ethnologue were especially helpful, since they are sites that deal with an overview of all the world's languages. Omniglot was especially useful, as its biggest focus is all of the world's writing systems both past and present.

For the first chapter, the literature was not as plentiful as one would have hoped. There were several websites—mainly for those learning English as a second language, but also run by English and linguistic departments at universities—that proved to be the most helpful. There were also some journal articles that discussed the history of the English language in general and, more specifically, the history of English orthography and phonetics. There was a lot more literature available for the final part of the first chapter, the part that dealt with previous attempts at spelling reform. First of all, there were numerous journal articles, articles in language—and sometimes specifically English—based journals. Some of these journals were contemporaneous, i.e. they were published at the time of the push for reform, even over one hundred years ago, whereas others discussed attempted reforms from decades prior. It was also not too difficult to find newspaper articles discussing this topic. Indeed, it is a topic that it seems that newspaper journalists enjoy occasionally writing about.

There was plenty of literature for the second chapter. For one thing, the transitions that other societies have made from one writing system to another have been well documented. There are plenty of newspaper articles, journal articles and websites that discuss that. The same thing can be said about spelling reforms in other languages. *The Guardian* and *The BBC* in particular have a number of articles discussing this.

The third chapter did not require as much literature. However, for what literature was required, the same journal articles that were so helpful in chapter one proved to be helpful in chapter three as well. Also, psychology articles proved useful for the discussion as to whether a more complicated orthography leads to dyslexia.

It was in chapter four for which the greatest variety of sources was required. The previously mentioned website, Omniglot, proved extremely helpful. For one thing, Omniglot shows the different orthographical systems in basically all of the European languages, and many of the world's non-European languages as well. Also in this chapter, textbooks and self-help study books for different languages were also quite helpful, with the *Colloquial* series (published by Routledge) being especially useful. It is also worth mentioning that these books were also useful in chapter two.

1.2. The History of the English Language – Brief Overview

English has a more unique history when compared to other European languages. For one thing, it could perhaps be called the original creole language. At this point, it is necessary to look at the definition of a creole language. The Creole language was initially defined as a language that developed on European plantation settlements throughout the 17th and 18th centuries, combining elements of European and local languages. The majority of these languages developed on the coasts of the Atlantic and Indian oceans (Accredited Language Services, 2019).

In more recent years, some linguists have expanded the definition of "Creole" to include languages that emerged due to contact between two non-European languages, rather than one European and one non-European tongue.

The key defining factor of all the various types of Creole is that they each developed as a means of communication between two mutually-unintelligible linguistic groups. For example, Standard French and the native languages of Haiti were eventually fused together to form Haitian Creole. Creole languages tend to develop in isolated areas, especially on islands like Haiti (Accredited Language Services, 2019).

In the sense that a creole language is a combination of several mutually unintelligible languages, English could be called a creole language. After all, modern English emerged in the High Middle Ages as a combination of Anglo-Saxon and Norman French. Anglo-Saxon was itself a combination of several different Germanic languages, namely Old Norse from Scandinavia and various dialects from modern day Germany and the Netherlands:

> "The history of the English language really started with the arrival of three Germanic tribes who invaded Britain during the 5th century AD. These tribes, the Angles, the Saxons and the Jutes, crossed the North Sea from what today is Denmark and northern Germany. At that time the inhabitants of Britain spoke a Celtic language. But most of the Celtic speakers were pushed west and north by the

invaders - mainly into what is now Wales, Scotland and Ireland" (English Club, 2019).

As was previously mentioned, the history of the English language took a dramatic turn when the French-speaking Normans arrived in England in 1066:

> *"Middle English (1100-circa 1500 AD):* After William the Conqueror, the Duke of Normandy [who spoke French], invaded and conquered England in 1066 AD...The Old French took over as the language of the court, administration, and culture...The English language, as the language of the now lower class, was considered a vulgar tongue. By about 1200, England and France had split. English changed a lot, because it was mostly being spoken instead of written for about 300 years. The use of Old English came back, but with many French words added. This language is called Middle English... Because the English underclass cooked for the Norman upper class, the words for most domestic animals are English (*ox, cow, calf, sheep, swine, deer*) while the words for the meats derived from them are French (*beef, veal, mutton, pork, bacon, venison*)" (Study English Today, 2019).

As one can see, English is the result of a combination of a number of different, mutually unintelligible languages, from two different branches, Germanic and Romance, of the Indo-European language family. Indeed, one could add a third branch, as there are Celtic influences in English as well. As a result of this, English has one of the world's largest vocabularies. For example, English has the word "people" from the French "peuple", and "folks" from the German "volk" (also "folk" in Swedish). As is often the case, when one word is of French origin and the other is of German, the French word is considered the more formal. Part of the reason that English spelling is more cumbersome is because the words originated in different languages, which had different orthographies for the Latin alphabet.

It is worth noting that it is partly as a result of this merger of several languages that English ended up with a simpler grammar structure. One final note on the history of English: since it has a simpler grammar structure, it is easier to create new words. Indeed, English is quicker to create new words than other languages: some examples include "smog" from "smoke" and "fog" and "motel" from "motorway" and "hotel":

Every year, about 1,000 new English words come into use. The English language is fast at adapting to the changing world and, as it evolves, these new words appear from many different walks of life (Zazulak, 2016).

1.2.1. The History of English Pronunciation and Orthography

Before considering an improved way to spell the English language, it is necessary to take a brief look as to how English orthography became the way it is and how it became one of the least phonetical European languages using the Latin alphabet. It is not, however, necessary to focus too heavily on this, as it is more important to focus on how to solve this issue, rather than how the issue came to be in the first place.

As one can see, the English language is an interesting combination of several other European languages. As a result, the orthography is also a combination and is therefore not as regular:

> "Tongues and ears aren't the only lazy things. Scribes and typesetters can be, too. If you bring over scribes from France or typesetters from the Netherlands and Belgium, where the first presses in Britain came from, they will tend to the standards they're used to. The French scribes, with their Latin influence, didn't see why we would write *cwen* when obviously what they heard should be spelled something like *queen*. The Dutch typesetters felt that *gost* was missing something, so they slipped in an h to make *ghost*" (Harbeck, 2015).

Moreover, the orthographic system has not changed much since the High Middle Ages. However, the pronunciation has changed considerably, more so than in other European languages. The most notable example of this is the great vowel shift, which occurred towards the end of the High Middle Ages and into the Early Modern Era:

> "A major factor separating Middle English from Modern English is known as the Great Vowel Shift, a radical change in pronunciation during the 15th, 16th and 17th Century, as a result of which long vowel sounds began to be made higher and further forward in the mouth (short vowel sounds were largely unchanged). In fact, the shift probably started very gradually some centuries before 1400, and continued long after 1700 (some subtle changes arguably continue even to this day). Many languages have undergone vowel shifts, but the major changes of the English vowel shift occurred within the relatively short space of a century or two, quite a sudden and dramatic shift in linguistic terms.

It was largely during this short period of time that English lost the purer vowel sounds of most European languages, as well as the phonetic pairing between long and short vowel sounds" (The History of English, 2019).

These changes in pronunciation continue to the present day:

> "The pronunciation of the word *tunes* is here is very revealing. Many older speakers in the UK would pronounce a <y> sound in between the initial consonant and vowel of a word like *tune* or *dune*—so that they sound like 'tyoon' and 'dyoon' respectively. Younger speakers are far more likely to blend the consonant and <y> sound into a <ch> and <j> sound respectively. Thus the word *tune* might sound something like 'choon' and the word *dune* might be pronounced like '*June*'...
>
> Some changes merely affect the way a single word is pronounced: older speakers across the UK tend to stress the first syllable in the word *controversy*, for instance, while younger speakers increasingly place the main stress on the second syllable, *controversy*" (British Library , 2019).

Another good example of a pronunciation change is the "r" in "br" combinations becoming silent in some words. While it is still not unheard of for people to pronounce the "r" in "February", it has become quite uncommon and the "r" has become silent most of the time. As a related example. it is also not uncommon for people to fail to pronounce the "r" in "library", though the majority do. It is indeed possible to foresee a time in the future when this letter also becomes silent. Another good example of pronunciation change is in the "nt" combination. In American English, the "t" is increasingly becoming silent. As a result, "interesting" is increasingly becoming "inneresting".

1.2.3. Previous Attempts at Spelling Reform in English

The idea that we should have spelling reform in English is not a new one:

> "The indications are that spelling reform is one of those time-worn phrases the use of which tends to prevent a calm scrutiny of the facts. It seems to excite in many minds on both sides of the ocean a psychical reaction which is unfavorable to sober discussion. It calls up images of a dear mother-tongue mutilated and made hideous by soulless vandals; of a demand that men and women who have once learned to read and spell shall acquire these useful arts over again" (Calvin, 1902, p. 297).

As one can see, the term "spelling reform" was already being called "time-worn" in 1902, well over a hundred years ago. In one sense, this is not surprising, considering that the first known call for spelling reform occurred back in the sixteenth century:

> "The Great Vowels Shift changed all that; by the end of the sixteenth century the "e" in "sheep" sounded like that in Modern English "sheep" or "meet"...To many it seemed that the pronunciation had moved so far from its visual representation that a new alphabet was needed, and in the sixteenth century we have the first attempts to "reform" English spellings, a movement still active today. In 1569 John Hart (in his *Orthographie*) went so far as to devise a new phonetic alphabet to remedy what he considered a fatal flaw in our system of language. (His alphabet and the work of other language reformers provides us with our best

9

evidence for the pronunciation of English in his time)" (Harvard, 2019).

One very notable early attempt at spelling reform in English came from the late eighteenth century, with Benjamin Franklin, one of the Founding Fathers of the United States of America, as one of the leading voices in its favor:

> "Benjamin Franklin took great interest in the promotion of spelling reform. While living in London in 1768 he wrote *A Scheme for a new Alphabet and a Reformed Mode of Spelling* in which he proposed a fairly accurate phonetic system for spelling English. The alphabet was published in 1779 in Franklin's *Political, Miscellaneous, and Philosophical Pieces.*
>
> His new phonetic alphabet consisted all the lowercase letters of the Latin alphabet, minus c, j, q, w, x, and y, which he thought redundant, plus six new letters for sounds which he thought lacked unambiguous orthographic representation. The other letters all adhered to the principle of one symbol (or unique digraph) per sound.
>
> Franklin commissioned a type foundry to prepare a suitable type including for the 6 new letters, but soon lost interest in his alphabet" (Omniglot, 2019).

While it is obvious why he would have considered the letters "c", "q", and "x" to be redundant, it is hard to see why he would have considered the other three letters as redundant, as they are vital for English.

The turn of the century (i.e. the final decades of the nineteenth century and initial decades of the twentieth century) was a particularly strong time in calls for spelling reform in English. George Bernard Shaw is famous for having suggested "ghoti" as an alternative spelling for "fish". However, the *New York Times* claims that, like a lot of famous quotes, it is a misquote, or at a minimum there is no evidence that he ever actually said it:

> The Irish playwright George Bernard Shaw is said to have joked that the word 'fish' could legitimately be spelled 'ghoti,' by using the 'gh' sound from 'enough,' the 'o' sound from 'women' and the 'ti' sound from 'action.'

Just one problem with the well-worn anecdote: there's not a shred of evidence that Shaw, though a noted advocate for spelling reform, ever brought up *ghoti*. Scholars have searched high and low through Shaw's writings and have never found him suggesting *ghoti* as a comical respelling of *fish*.

The true origins of *ghoti* go back to 1855, before Shaw was even born. In December of that year, the publisher Charles Ollier sent a letter to his good friend Leigh Hunt, a noted poet and literary critic. "My son William has hit upon a new method of spelling 'Fish,' " Ollier wrote. You guessed it: good old *ghoti* (Zimmer, 2010).

As the quote implies, the origin of "ghoti" as an alternative spelling for fish must predate even 1855, if it was already "good old" by then. As was previously stated, the late nineteenth century saw a notable peak in interest in the concept of spelling reform. Indeed, a quick search for "spelling reform" will reveal numerous articles written in the 1870s and 1880s. *The Journal of Education*, *New England Journal of Education*, and *National Journal of Education* all published articles on this topic.

It is actually quite surprising—and disappointing—how little progress has been made with regards to this issue, especially when one considers how many famous and influential people have been involved in this movement. The Simplified Spelling Board was founded in the United States in 1906. The SSB's original 30 members consisted of authors, professors and dictionary editors. Andrew Carnegie, a founding member, supported the SSB with yearly bequests of more than US$300,000. In April 1906, it published a list of 300 words, which included 157 spellings that were already in common use in American English.

A number of famous names have been involved in reforming the English spelling system over the centuries, but probably one of the most unexpected names on that list is Theodore Roosevelt. Known for his uncompromising stance on many issues, in the early 1900s Roosevelt used the full power of his position to try to force through several hundred new spelling reforms in an attempt to make the language—and the cost of printing government documents—more economical. Despite even the president's involvement, however, in the end Roosevelt's war on spelling collapsed before it was able to have any lasting effect on our spelling (Jones, 2016).

Jones's article goes on to note other famous proponents of spelling reform, such as Benjamin Franklin (who has already been mentioned) along with Andrew Carnegie, Noah Webster, and Brigham Young. Indeed, a spelling reform board was created and Carnegie managed to raise a considerable amount of money for it. Jones claims that in the end, the effort failed largely due to the backlash

Roosevelt received from what were perceived as having been heavy handed tactics. One other noteworthy point Jones makes includes the fact Noah Webster was motivated more by his desire to see a break between the variants of English in the United States and the United Kingdom, rather than a genuine desire to simplify the spelling system. Indeed, some of the most notable differences between British and American spelling can be traced back to Webster. For example, the elimination of the extra "u" in words such as "neighbor" and "favor" and the use of "er" instead of "re" in words such as "center" and "meter".

Conclusions to Chapter 1

As can be seen, a variety of sources were available on this topic. These sources came in a number of different forms: books, journals, newspaper articles (many of which are nowadays posted online), and websites. These sources adequately covered all the various issues regarding this topic: the history of the English language, the history of English pronunciation and orthography, previous attempts at spelling reform in English, and spelling reforms in other languages.

As for the history of English: English truly has one of the most unique histories of any European language. While it is not uncommon for European languages, like languages in other parts of the world, to borrow heavily from other languages—including those to which they bear little to no relation—probably no other European language can be considered a creole, especially since the root languages come from two different branches—Germanic and Romance—of the Indo-European family of languages. Indeed, one could even add a third one, Celtic, if one takes into consideration the

Welsh influences on English. Needless to say, such a unique history for the English language makes the English language one of Europe's more unique ones.

As was mentioned, a combination of several different orthographic traditions contributed to the current situation and goes a long way in explaining why English has such a cumbersome orthographic system. Moreover, while many languages do experience some change in pronunciation over time, English in particular has experienced a huge shift in pronunciation, notably the great vowel shift of the High Middle Ages. The spelling system, however, did not shift in order to take this change into account. These factors combined to create the current cumbersome system.

Since the system is so cumbersome, there have been previous attempts at spelling reform. Indeed, the first one was noted in the sixteenth century. The most notable one occurred about 100 years ago. It is truly a shame that none of these attempts were successful.

CHAPTER 2. SPELLING REFORMS IN OTHER LANGUAGES

Introduction to Chapter 2

English is not the only language to have dealt with the issue of spelling reform. Indeed, a quick search of the term "spelling reform" shows that numerous languages have undergone some form of spelling reform at some point in their histories. Some of these reforms have been quite recent—i.e. within the last few decades—and some were over five centuries ago. In order to see what a possible reform in English would look like, it is helpful to see how it went in other languages. What follows in this chapter is a very brief overview of spelling reforms in other languages. Obviously, this will not be an exhaustive list of spelling reforms in other languages.

1.3.2.1. Change in Writing Systems

At this point, it is necessary to make a distinction between spelling reform and change in writing systems. The former involves keeping the same writing system (usually an alphabet), whereas the latter involves going from one writing system to another. Theoretically, any change in writing systems is possible, but usually it involves either going from a non-alphabet writing system to an alphabet or from one alphabet to another. Even though this study is not suggesting that English be written in any other writing system and is instead suggesting a reform of the manner in which English is written in the Latin alphabet, it would still be interesting to very briefly explore instances where other languages have gone from being written in one writing system to another.

Before mentioning notable examples of changes in writing systems, it is worth noting why certain languages are written with the writing system that is used and why that system is changed. One of the most influential features in the choice of a writing system involves religion. This is not surprising as religion—along with language—is usually one of the most important factors in a given society's culture and identity.

A really great example of this phenomenon (i.e. religion influencing the choice of writing system) is the choice of alphabet in the various European countries. With a few notable exceptions, if a European country is either Catholic or Protestant, then its language is written using the Latin alphabet. If a European country is Orthodox, then the alphabet used is anything but Latin: Russia, Bulgaria, Belarus, Ukraine, and North Macedonia all write their languages (and in the case of Russia, numerous other often completely unrelated languages within its borders, such as Chechen) using the Cyrillic alphabet; Greece uses the Greek alphabet; Georgia uses the Georgian alphabet; and Armenia[1] uses the Armenian alphabet.

The most notable exception to this is Romania, an Orthodox country where the Latin alphabet is used. This is unsurprising given that Romanian is itself a Latin-based

---

[1] The Armenian Apostolic Church is not technically Orthodox, as it is a separate entity. However, in this context Armenia can be counted in with the Orthodox countries of Europe.

language. However, even in the instance of the Romanian language, the Cyrillic alphabet was used in the past. Indeed, there is evidence to believe that the Cyrillic alphabet was the first one used to write Romanian:

> "Romanian first appeared in writing during the 16th century, mainly in religious texts and other documents. The earliest known text in Romanian, which dates from 1521, is a letter from Neacşu of Câmpulung to the mayor of Braşov. Neacşu wrote in a version of the old Cyrillic alphabet similar to the one for Old Church Slavonic, which was used in Walachia and Moldova until 1859.
>
> From the late 16th century a version of the Latin alphabet using Hungarian spelling conventions was used to write Romanian in Translyvania. Then in the late 18th century a spelling system based on Italian was adopted" (Omniglot, 2019).

The Cyrillic alphabet was also used during Soviet times to write the Romanian language in Moldova. It is worth noting that while the Soviet authorities imposed Cyrillic on Romanian in Moldova, they did not impose it on the Catholic/Protestant Baltic states, as they continued to write their respective languages in the Latin alphabet. This difference is particularly noteworthy when one considers the fact that the Soviet Union was anti-religion and would most likely have not been interested in a Catholic/Protestant versus Orthodox heritage issue with regards to the choice of alphabet. So important was the change back to the Latin alphabet in Moldova that there is actually a street in Chişinău named after the day in 1989 when the Soviet authorities permitted the Moldovans to change back to writing the Romanian language in the Latin alphabet.

One other possible exception to this church-based choice of whether to use the Latin alphabet within Europe is the Serbo-Croatian language:

> "The historical division of the South Slav lands between the Orthodox and Catholic spheres of influence has meant that the Serbian and Croatian language may be written in either the Cyrillic or the Latin script. Both have been modified for the language's phonetic system, and transliteration letter for letter is possible from one to the other" (Hawkesworth, 1998, p. 2).

It is important to note that people argue as to whether there is a single Serbo-Croatian language. While there are some notable differences between say, the variants used in Croatia versus Serbia, it has been said that the differences are more political rather than linguistic. Unsurprisingly, the language is written exclusively with the Latin alphabet in Catholic Croatia. However, in the case of Orthodox Serbia, both the Cyrillic and the Latin alphabets are used. It is quite remarkable that the Serbo-Croatian language is very phonetic in both alphabets and that 30 Cyrillic letters have an exact one or two-letter equivalent in the Latin alphabet.

One final note about religion and the choice of alphabet in Europe: Albania. Albania is both Muslim and Christian and amongst the Christians, both the Catholic and Orthodox Churches are prominent (Catholic more in the north and Orthodox more in the south). In the case of Albania, there is therefore no clear choice of alphabet with regard to religion. Albanian is therefore unsurprisingly written with the Latin alphabet. Unsurprising given that that is the world's most prominent writing system.

In addition, it is worth mentioning that even the one notable Orthodox country outside of Europe, Ethiopia, also does not use the Latin alphabet, as they use the Ge'ez syllabic alphabet. Indeed, it seems as if Orthodox countries—with the notable exception of Romania, whose language is Latin-based—insist on writing with anything but the Latin alphabet.

Europe is not the only place where the dominant religion is a major factor in the choice of a writing system. Another very noteworthy example is the Muslim world. Oftentimes, countries that are predominately Muslim will write their respective languages using the Arabic abjad, regardless of the linguistic background of the language in question or the part of the world in which the country in question is located. Examples of the Arabic abjad being used to write unrelated languages include Farsi, Pashtun, and Urdu. It has also historically been used to write other languages in Muslim dominated parts of the world, such as in Malaysia, Kazakhstan, Turkey, and amongst Muslim majority, ethnic minorities in countries such as Russia and India.

Religion is not the only strong factor with regard to the choice of, and sometimes change, in the writing system. Another factor is geographic location, along with previous historical ties. As was already stated, many of the languages of Russia, most of which have little in common with Russian, are written using the Cyrillic alphabet. This is in spite of the fact that some of these ethnic groups are not predominately Orthodox Christian. Russian influence is also the reason why the Turkic languages of Central Asia, along with Mongolian are (or in some cases were) written with the Cyrillic alphabet.

One of the biggest reasons why the Latin alphabet is so widespread is because of the historical empires of Western European countries, such as Britain, France, the Netherlands, Spain, and Portugal, among others. All of these countries write their respective languages using the Latin alphabet. As a result of this, numerous languages in Asia, Africa, the Pacific, and the Americas are written with the Latin alphabet.

One factor that is not all that common in the choice of a writing system, though probably should be, is how suited a given writing system is to the language in question. The reason Atatürk switched Turkish from the Arabic abjad to the Latin alphabet was that he both wanted to orient Turkey towards Europe and also to de-emphasize Islam. However, even though it probably was not his motive, the Latin alphabet is far more efficient for spelling Turkish than the Arabic abjad, because vowel harmony is an important aspect in the Turkish language and abjads do not show or only weakly show vowels:

> "Its intrinsic beauty aside, there is nothing to be said in favour of the Arabo-Persian alphabet as a medium for writing Turkish. All of its letters, including alif the glottal stop, are consonants, some representing sounds not existing in Turkish and one, ky which may represent Turkish g, ky ny or y. The sound of η indicated by the Arabo-Persian k was originally /ng/, pronounced as in English singer, in scholarly transcriptions of old texts it is usually shown by. It occurs in such Ottoman spellings as kwkl for gönül 'soul', and dkz or dkyz for deniz 'sea'. It is still heard in some Turks' pronunciation of sonra 'after'. With the addition of diacritics above or below the letters, the three vowels a, i, and u can be indicated, whereas Turkish needs to distinguish eight. The Arabic letters alif wäwy and yâ were

employed in Arabic and Persian to show ä, üy and t respectively. In Turkish they were used to indicate a/ey o/ö/u/üy and i/ay/ey respectively" (Lewis, 1999, p. 27).

There have been several other recent changes in writing systems. Interestingly, they also mainly involve Turkic languages, such as Azeri and Kazakh. They have mostly occurred amongst the newly independent countries that emerged as a result of the collapse of the Soviet Union. In these instances, it was the same change: from the Cyrillic alphabet to the Latin alphabet. The reason for the use of the Cyrillic alphabet was due to the Russian influence. It is important to remember that these areas were under the control of Tsarist Russia prior to the Soviet era.

The motive for the change is often that they wanted to come out from Russian influence and leaving the Cyrillic alphabet was a way to at least symbolically do that. Also, the Latin alphabet has become by far the most common one used around the world, for reasons stated above. Indeed, modern technology is one of the factors in Kazakhstan's decision to switch. Part of the latest switch relates to modern technology. The Cyrillic alphabet has 42 symbols, making it cumbersome to use with digital devices – a standard Kazakh keyboard utilises almost all number keys in addition to letter and punctuation keys.

The new proposed Latin alphabet works around that by using apostrophe signs to modify letters. The country's official name would thus be spelled as Qazaqstan Respy'blikasy (Reuters, 2017).

From a purely linguistic point of view, the Latin alphabet is not necessarily more efficient for writing these

Turkic languages than the Cyrillic alphabet is, though the fact that the Kazakh version has 42 letters does indicate a certain level of inefficiency. Therefore, as is often the case, the decision was based more on geopolitics rather than linguistics. It's important to note that having separate writing systems helps to maintain the world's linguistic diversity. Moreover, the Cyrillic alphabet need not be associated with Russia. After all, it was invented by Bulgarian monks living in present-day Greece. Having stated all of that, there is certainly nothing wrong with these countries using the Latin alphabet to write their Turkic languages.

This brings up the issue of writing systems that are no longer in use: some notable examples include the Mongolian script, Runic, Hungarian Runes, and several writing systems from Southeast Asia. For example, prior to using the Latin alphabet, indigenous writing systems existed in the Southeast Asia countries of Indonesia, Vietnam, and the Philippines. Some of these writing systems are still used for decoration or ceremonial purposes. Losing writing systems, like losing languages, decreases the world's linguistic diversity:

> "There have always been far more languages than scripts. And languages have disappeared far more readily than scripts. Often a script has continued in widespread use by virtue of being adapted to a new language, sometimes more than once. This is what happened to cuneiform, to Chinese characters and to the Greek alphabet, but not significantly, to Egyptian and Mayan hieroglyphs.
>
> The reason why a script survives or perishes is not obvious. Sign simplicity or efficiency in representing the sounds of a language cannot be the sole criteria of survival. If they were, Chinese characters would have disappeared in China

and been replaced by an alphabet; and the Japanese would never have borrowed Chinese characters. Political and economic power, religious and cultural prestige and the existence of a major literature all play a part in the historical fate of a script" (Robinson, 2007, p. 69).

1.4.2.2. Changes within the Same Writing System

The previous sub-chapter discussed languages undergoing a change in writing system, usually from a non-alphabet to an alphabet, or from one alphabet to another. However, it is far more common that a language maintains the same writing system—usually an alphabet—and instead changes the manner in which that language is spelled in the same alphabet. This is the case with regards to the proposed spelling reform for English.

A good example of spelling reform in a non-Latin alphabet, European language is Greek. Indeed, Greek—like Georgian and Armenian—has its own alphabet that no other language uses. It is important to note, though, that the Greek alphabet has historically been used to write both the Albanian and Ossetian languages, just as the Georgian alphabet has historically been used to write both the Ossetian and Abkhazian languages.

In the case of Greek, there was not just the issue of how best to spell the language, but also what the official, standard dialect should be:

> "Greece, occupied by the Turks, adopted many loan words from the Turkish language. Even now the majority of foreign words in the Greek language are of Turkish, or

Latin, origin. The development of the spoken and written forms of the Greek language continued during this period. At the same time an 'accepted' written form of the spoken language was introduced. This, however, failed altogether.

At the end of this period, a pure form of the language, free of loan words developed. It largely resembled an archaic form of Classic Greek; it was incomprehensible, to a certain degree, to most Greeks! This 'puristic' form came to be known as *Katharevusa*...

Athenian Greek grew as the standard spoken 'popular' language from around 1880, and for the next 30 years this language was the established literary language. Athenian Greek also became the official school language, despite fierce opposition from the Katharevusa followers. This standard spoken language (Athenian Greek) was called Demotic (meaning 'popular', or used by the 'population') ...

1976 Demotic was proclaimed the official school language.

1977 Demotic was proclaimed the official language of Greece.

And finally in 1982, the accent system was officially limited to one accent on a word" (Matsukas, 1997, pp. 3-4).

That last sentence brings up a key point: prior to the 1982 spelling reform, it was not uncommon for a word to have several different diacritics. Some of these marks even indicated things such as where to breathe. One of the main reasons why these were dropped is because they were largely needless:

"The signs for the "breathing" of initial vowels...can be ignored" (Berlitz, 1985, p. 114).

Today, the one accent mark per word, which is always an acute accent, shows the syllable upon which the stress is supposed to fall. In the end, it is worth noting that the Greek alphabet is not one of the more efficient alphabets. For example, there are only twenty-four letters. Of these twenty-four letters, three of them, the "η", "ι", and the "υ", all spell the same sound, the Greek equivalent of a long "e" sound in English. Indeed, there are even half a dozen other, two-vowel combinations to spell that same sound, just in case having three different letters for the same sound was not enough. Likewise, the "Ο" and "ω" both spell the same sound, the Greek equivalent of the English "o".

The reverse is also true: Greek lacks a single letter to spell the equivalents of the English sounds "b", "d", "j", "ch", and "sh". Instead, those sounds are spelled "μπ", "ντ", "τζ", "τσ", and "σ", respectively, albeit English lacks a single letter to spell those last two sounds as well. Indeed, many other languages that use the Latin alphabet use diacritics on single letters to spell those sounds (more on this in chapter 4).

Oftentimes, spelling reform merely means dropping letters that are no longer useful. This was the case in the Georgian language, a language that has its own alphabet. In fact, not only does Georgia have its own alphabet, it in essence has had three different alphabets, as there are two older versions of the current Georgian alphabet. The first manifestation of this alphabet was one which contained purely capital letters. This variety of the xucuri script is known as Asomtavruli, 'capital'...

After some centuries another form of the xucuri script known as nusxuri or 'lower-case' emerged...By the time the eleventh century came to pass, these ecclesiastical forms of the alphabet were replaced by a single "new" alphabet called mxedruli (pronounced mkhe-dru-lee) meaning 'military.'...In modern times, the alphabet has been slightly modified to exclude certain letters whose phonemes have disappeared from the language. Thus, the mxedruli alphabet has changed from 39 to 33 letters (mostly dropping diphthongs). The current Georgian alphabet has five vowels and 28 consonants (Jorgensen, 2000).

Some of the languages using the Cyrillic alphabet have also undergone spelling reform. Two notable examples of this are Bulgarian and Russian. Shortly after the Soviet takeover of Russia, the authorities implemented a reform known as the Sovnarkom decree, which came into force in October of 1918. Russian philologist and historian Aleksey Shakhmatov organized the Assembly for Implementing Simplification of the Orthography, according to it there were formulated new rules soon adopted by the Ministry of Popular Education. In December 1917 the People's Commissariat of Education issued a decree which stated that all state and government institutions and schools had to implement the transition to the new orthography without delay, all government and state publications, both periodical and non-periodical were to be printed in the new style. In this way, the new radical authorities along with almost everything in the vast country rejected the old-fashioned alphabet as well. If someone accustomed to modern Russian picks up any publication that's more than 100 years old, they are immediately struck by the mass of unfamiliar symbols: the silly-looking Ѣ/ѣ (yat'), the **Latin-like *i***, the excess ъ, not to mention a few unusual spelling choices for common endings. Once the initial shock passes, however, it turns out that the publication is quite readable, even as the rules for using these extra letters remain baffling, even mysterious (Sokolskaya, 2013).

The article goes on to mention that as a result of the reformed spelling, *War and Peace* became eleven pages shorter. However, it must be emphasized that in spite of having undergone a spelling reform within the last 100 years, Russian is still not one of Europe's more phonetical languages. For example, the "г" in "его" is pronounced more as a "в". Also, vowel sounds shift depending on the syllable upon which the stress falls. In this sense, one could say that the 1918 reform was a failure. In fact, so much so that there was talk in Soviet times about a continuation of spelling reform:

> "On 24 March 1962, Izvestija ran an article by A. I. Efimov entitled *Eloquence and Orthography*, in which the author claims that in Russian schools orthography has killed eloquence. He explains that the time allotted for study of Russian is taken up mainly in learning orthography and all the rules of exceptions, unjustified illogical details, variants and intricate traps, which strongly smell of "medieval scholastics"...
>
> After pointing out that it was difficult to completely carry out the reform of Russian orthography in 1917-1918 due to the general situation caused by the war, he demands that this reform be undertaken now without any further delay" (Klein, 1964, p. 54).

As one can see, the European languages written with the Latin alphabet are not the only ones to have undergone spelling reform. Likewise, as one can also see, spelling reform also often means dropping letters that are no longer useful, as once happened in English as well. However, at this point it is necessary to review some of the European languages written in the Latin alphabet which have undergone spelling reform. After all, this is the situation English is in.

As was previously mentioned, Greek faced this issue of which variant of the language should be the standard. Other languages have faced a similar issue. As the above-mentioned quote stated, oftentimes the dispute is about which regional variant to use, or the level of formality. While it is not the focus of this research to explore such issues—after all, the issue here is about making the spelling system more faithful to how English is pronounced today, and not which variant of English should be used as a standard variety—there is one other noteworthy example to mention: Norwegian:

> "The majority language, *Norwegian*, has two distinct written varieties: *Bokmål* ('Book Language') and *Nynorsk* ('New Norwegian'). They are so close to each other linguistically that they may be regarded as «written dialects», mutually completely intelligible. Orally, local dialects are extensively used throughout the country. They are also mutually intelligible, although they can be very diverse, not least in intonation. In addition, both Swedish and Danish are closely related to Norwegian and thus intelligible to Norwegians, although with some initial difficulty in many cases.
>
> In speech, there is much blending between dialects, Bokmål and Nynorsk, but in writing, the varieties are kept more clearly apart. Nynorsk is mostly used in Western Norway as a written language (by roughly 10 % of the people, amounting to about half a million), Bokmål is

dominant in the rest of the country, and is used in writing by close to 90%" (Språkrådet, 2109).

As one can see, the differences between the two varieties of Norwegian are actually "written dialects", as they are not based on spoken variations, but rather a dispute on the best way to spell the Norwegian language. The reason came to be as a result of the Black Death of the fourteenth century. Nearly every literate person in Norway died. As a result of being in a union with Denmark, Danish scribes were brought in. Indeed, Danish became the spoken language of much of the elite in Norway. It was only after Norway was transferred to Sweden that interest in a revival of the written Norwegian began:

Arguments were based on three different positions.

1. Keep the Danish.
2. Develop a new written language based on the Norwegian dialects.
3. Norwegianize the Danish

The first alternative was rejected. The two others were both set into practice. Ivar Aasen (1813-1896), a linguist and poet with a rural background, developed *Landsmål*, as it was called, based on extensive research on rural dialects in western and central parts of southern Norway. In 1929 it was labelled *Nynorsk* – *"New Norwegian"* which still is used. *Landsmål* became an official norm in 1885…During the next 50 years, the language was widely accepted, but did never obtain a position as the language for the majority.

Knud Knudsen (1812-1895), a grammarian and headmaster, had the goal of altering Danish orthography until it reflected the informal speech of the educated classes in Norway. *Riksmål* was established as a norm by a spelling reform in 1907. In 1929 this variant was labelled *"Bokmål"* – *"Book language"*. During the 20th century a succession of spelling reforms led to the inclusion of forms related to lower urban class and rural speech in Bokmål...

It became a political goal to fuse *Nynorsk* and *Bokmål* into one form, *Samnorsk (Common Norwegian)*. This idea was abandoned in the 1960s, *Nynorsk* and *Bokmål* have developed as two parallel written forms of Norwegian (Norwegian on the Web, 2019).

Under the law in Norway, both written variants have official status and all legislation is supposed to be published in both. This is a key issue with regards to spelling reform in English: would English-speaking countries end up with two different written variants being used simultaneously and if so, would that cause confusion (more on this in the next chapter)?

There are a number of other European languages using the Latin alphabet which have undergone spelling reform. A good example is French. The spelling reform of French has a number of parallels to English. First of all, the reform is recent, as it began in 1990. Also, French, like English, is spoken in different countries on different continents. Moreover, French, like English, is one of Europe's least phonetical languages.

When the reform began, it received little attention and basically got nowhere:

"You'd be forgiven for not realising, but French has had a spelling reform. Or at least, reforms to the French spelling system, originally proposed in 1990 but largely ignored, have recently seen fresh impetus. Various French dictionaries and spellcheckers are now including the reformed spellings, and the new spellings are supposedly being taught in French-speaking primary schools. It is fair to say that for the time being at least, real-life use of the reformed spellings in actual French publications is marginal and as we'll see, opinion about them is somewhat divided. Nonetheless, it is worth being aware of the proposals, as over the coming years we are likely to see more of a mixture of new and old spellings being used and potentially expected" (Coffey, 2017).

However, once it was announced that the reforms were to be implemented in French school textbooks in 2016, it stirred outrage:

> "It went unnoticed again last autumn. But the news this month that school manuals will incorporate changes to the spelling of 2,400 words next autumn [2016] ignited passions.
>
> It's ironic that the spelling flap is propagated by social media, which daily perpetrate countless outrages against the French and English languages.
>
> I'm not upset about the transformation of *oignon* (onion) to *ognon*, or that *nénuphar* is returning to *nénufar*. (The Persian word was changed in 1935 to make it closer to *nymphéa*, which also means water lily.)
>
> But I admit a certain sympathy for protesters who tweet under the hashtag #JeSuisCirconflexe, an expression of solidarity with the accent, and an echo of the "Je Suis

Charlie" slogan that followed the January 2015 jihadist attacks.

The circumflex will be removed from the letters "i" and "u".

The endearing tent or hat-shaped mark denotes the "s" that followed vowels in old French" (Marlowe, 2016).

French speakers in the various French speaking countries, such as Belgium and Quebec, have begun to slowly incorporate the new spellings, such as in newspapers. It is hard to tell whether opposition to the new spelling was based on resistance to the idea of spelling reform in general, or to the specific proposals themselves. Indeed, it could be said that this proposed reform seems to miss the point. After all, this reform seems to be more about diacritics—notably the hyphen and the circumflex—rather than changes in spelling, though there are some words that will have a new spelling, with "onion" ("ognon" rather than "oignon") being a notable example.

In French, as in English, there can often be a number of different ways to spell the same sound. However, unlike in English, in French, there are usually not different ways to pronounce the same spelling. As a result, it has been said in French that it is hard to guess the spelling of a spoken word, but it's easy to guess the pronunciation of a written word. This reform does not seem to improve this situation in French much. By contrast, the situation with regards to hyphens and circumflexes really did not need to be improved. This is an important lesson with regards to any attempt at spelling reform in English: no reform is better than a reform that is either bad or pointless.

Another good example of a recent spelling reform of a European language using the Latin alphabet is Portuguese. Portuguese, like English, is a European language spoken in a number of different countries on different continents. Also, like English, Portuguese is not one of Europe's more phonetical languages. However, in the case of Portuguese, standardization seems to be more the motive rather than a spelling system faithful to the spoken word:

Portuguese has had new rules in place since Wednesday 13th May, 2015.

The rules are supposed to apply to all the countries where Portuguese is the official language…

The Portuguese Language Orthographic Agreement (Portuguese abbreviation: NaO) was signed in 1990 and began being implemented in 2009…

The NaO agreement's main goal is to standardise the sixth most spoken language in the world…

The Portuguese written word is being brought closer to the spoken word, creating a unified spelling to be used in all Portuguese-speaking countries.

NaO was signed by official representatives of Angola, Brazil, Cape Verde, Guinea-Bissau, Mozambique, Portugal and São Tomé and Príncipe. Timor-Leste signed in 2004. Angola and Mozambique have not yet ratified it.

Until NaO, orthographic rules differed between Brazil and the other Portuguese-speaking countries (Lancashire, 2015).

In the case of the Portuguese reform, opposition to it seems to largely come from concern over cultural heritage. For example, many in Portugal have expressed a concern that the standard is too faithful to Brazil. Also, some people in Portuguese-speaking countries feel that any orthographic differences between these countries are an expression of cultural differences between them.

One other example to mention is that of German. German is a good example to look at, as it is a fellow Germanic language to English. As was the case with both French and Portuguese, German has also seen a recent reform in its spelling. As is also the case with French and Portuguese—not to mention English—German is also spoken in different countries. However, unlike the other three languages, German is only spoken on one continent, Europe. Also, unlike these other three languages, German was already one of Europe's more phonetical languages. As was the case with the other examples of spelling reform, this reform proved to be quite controversial. Indeed, it had been referred to as being "nearly a cultural war": Since 1st August 2006 the new spelling rules have been in force in Germany. The lead-up to it was plagued by a bitter dispute – proponents wanted to simplify the spelling rules, and critics feared a degeneration of the language.

"The spelling reform is as useful as a hole in the head," says Friedrich Denk. Today he is 73 years old, yet still sounds as belligerent as ever. He was among the most influential opponents of the spelling reform. As a teacher at a grammar school in Weilheim in Upper Bavaria, he was not willing to accept the new spelling... He was of the opinion that the reform denigrated the German language and, on top of that, would be expensive... He and other opponents of the reform primarily saw the intended simplification as a degeneration, a flattening, of the German language (Dittrich, 2019).

Since German was already such a phonetical language, the number of words affected by this change was far fewer than would be the case in English. Indeed, this German reform was more about technicalities like compound words, hyphens, and capitalization than about how faithful the spellings are to the spoken word. One of the highlights of the reform was clarification as to when to use the "ß". It is for these reasons that this reform was less necessary than a reform of English would be. In fact, this might actually have been the source of a fair amount of the controversy.

One final European language to mention with regards to spelling reform within the Latin alphabet: Swedish. Though not one of Europe's more phonetical languages, it is also not one of the least either. One notable example of where Swedish is not fully phonetical is the numerous ways that the [ɧ] sound can be spelled, examples include "sj" in sjö" "sk" in "skön" and "skj" in "skjorta". Also, there are some silent letters at the beginning of words, such as the "d" in "djur" and the "h" in "hjul". However, unlike the other languages mentioned, Swedish—at least in colloquial writing—is quicker to change the spelling of words in order to reflect new pronunciations. For example, the past tense of the verb "to say" is now often written as "sa" rather than "sade", since the "de" has mostly become silent. A hundred years ago, all four letters were pronounced. While this change is not official, it is becoming more common even in more formal writing.

Conclusions to Chapter 2

English is not the only language to have faced the issue of changing the manner in which its language is written. Indeed, many other languages have not merely undergone a reform of spelling, but a complete change from one writing system to another. Why a given society chooses a particular writing system—and consequently chooses to change its writing system—is often based on factors such as the dominate religion and historical connections to other parts of the world, rather than which writing system would be most efficient for spelling the language in question.

Probably the most famous example of a change in the writing system was around 100 years ago when Turkish went from being written with the Arabic abjad to the Latin alphabet. While the Latin alphabet is indeed more efficient for spelling Turkish, the motive was a desire to de-emphasize Islam and to connect Turkey to the West. Other examples of a change in writing systems include ex-Soviet states that are going from using the Cyrillic alphabet to the Latin one.

It is more common however, for obvious reasons, to reform the manner in which the words are spelled in the same writing system, rather than to change from one writing system to another. Such reforms have been seen in languages using different alphabets, such as Greek, Russian, Bulgarian, and Georgian.

There have been a number of examples—indeed, recent ones—of other Western European languages using the Latin alphabet to undergo spelling reform. In fact, English may actually be the unusual one for not having undergone such a reform, when it is English that needs it the most.

CHAPTER 3. THE PRACTICALITIES OF SPELLING REFORM

Introduction to Chapter 3

"I am heartily in favor of the reform in spelling, and shall hail the day when it shall be completely accomplished as the dawn of a grand advancement in education. How it shall be accomplished, is the puzzling question" (Powell, 1880).

After having very briefly reviewed both the history of the English language, with an especially close focus on the manner in which pronunciation has changed over time, along with examples of other languages having undergone a change in spelling (or indeed a change in writing system) it is now possible to examine the practicalities of spelling reform in English in the twenty-first century. This chapter shall discuss the pros and cons of spelling reform.

Professor Whitney gave what is probably the strongest argument in favor of spelling reform way back in 1876 at the annual meeting of the American Philological Association meeting in New York. He mentioned eight different points. The first two give the strongest arguments for spelling reform. The true and the sole office of alphabetical writing is faithfully and intelligibly to represent spoken speech, so-called "historical" orthography being only a con- cession to the weakness of prejudice. 2. The ideal of an alphabet is that every sound should have its own unvarying sign, and every sign, its own unvarying sound (Whitney, 1876).

The other six points mention other important factors such as the issue of whether any reforms should account for differences in regional dialects and the fact that the Latin alphabet was so well established in so many countries that any reform in English spelling would have to involve a change in, rather than a replacement of, the Latin alphabet.

This brings up the issue of practicalities with regards to spelling reform. This itself brings up the pros and cons of spelling reform.

1.5.3.1. The Positives of Spelling Reform

As always, it is best to start with the positives. The most obvious positive is that the new spelling system will more accurately reflect the manner in which the English language is actually spoken. After all, one of the big advantages of having an alphabet, as opposed to say, a character system like in China, or hieroglyphics like in Ancient Egypt or the Mayan world, is that it is supposed to give an exact account of how the words are to be pronounced. Many languages, including those written with the Latin alphabet, are so phonetical that a foreign speaker can easily tell how to pronounce the words in question with merely a scant knowledge of the orthography of the language in question. This includes German, a language closely related to English.

By contrast, in the case of English, it is common to see native English speakers with university degrees occasionally be unsure as to how to spell a word. Needless to say, that should not be happening. This would be unheard of in so many other languages. The fact that this is happening is an indication that the spelling system in English is broken.

Indeed, the fact that the "Spelling Bee" even exists is an indication of the problem.

The second biggest advantage of spelling reform is that it would make it easier for both children and non-native speakers to learn how to spell English. Moreover, many have suggested that dyslexia is more common amongst English-speaking children than children whose native language is more phonetical. However, there is research which disputes this claim:

> "The goal of the present study was to obtain a more precise description of dyslexia in different orthographies. The results clearly showed that the similarities between orthographies were far bigger than their differences. That is, dyslexics in both countries exhibited a reading speed deficit, a specific nonword reading deficit, and a phonological decoding mechanism that operates extremely slowly and serially. These problems were of similar size across orthographies and persisted even with respect to younger readers (i.e., reading level controls). The dyslexics in both countries did not show a major deficit in using body-size information, that is, both groups showed normal facilitatory body N effect compared to their controls" (Johannes C. Ziegler, 2003, p. 188).

However, it is important to note that the above-mentioned study only attempted to find how similar dyslexics with different native languages are. This particular study compared English-speaking dyslexics and German-speaking dyslexics. It did not attempt to determine whether dyslexia is more prevalent in countries where the language is less phonetical than in countries where the language is more phonetical. It is important to note that the study did find that there are some differences between English-speaking and German-speaking dyslexics. For one thing, the German-dyslexics seemed to show a somewhat greater accuracy. However, the authors are quick to urge caution on that point.

A study published several years prior to the above-mentioned one noted that dyslexia is indeed more common in children whose native languages are English or French rather than Italian: Research published in *Science* magazine suggests that parts of the brain crucial to reading are not working properly in dyslexics...

The study looked at why dyslexia is more common among English or French-speakers than Italians.

The English language is made up of just 40 sounds, but these can be spelt in more than 1000 different ways, say the researchers.

In Italian, the language's 25 sounds are made up in just 33 ways (BBC, 2001).

Interestingly, the authors of this research suggested that simplifying the orthographic system would be a good way to reduce the prevalence of dyslexia.

As was previously mentioned, one advantage of spelling reform is that it would make it easier for speakers of other languages to learn English. Seeing as how English has become by far the world's most important language, this is an important reason indeed. However, it must also be emphasized that languages should not, in and of themselves, be changed merely for the benefit of foreign speakers, as the language belongs first and foremost to the native speakers. After all, if this were the case then should grammar structures also be simplified in order to make it easier for people to learn English as a second language? That being said, simplifying the spelling system is not the same thing as purposely simplifying the grammar structure.

This brings up a key point: grammar rules and spelling are supposed to follow the natural language, and not the other way around. That's to say, grammar rules should include things that are not logical if that is what is said naturally. A good example of this is the Georgian language, where certain verbs such as "want (მინდა)" place the subject in the dative case and the direct object in the nominative case. Obviously, this defies logic, but it is the way in which it is naturally said by native Georgian-speakers, and Georgian-speakers should not force themselves to change the way they speak just because this notable aspect of Georgian grammar is illogical. Basically, the way things are actually said takes precedent over grammatical rules, which are supposed to follow the spoken language and not so much influence it. When people come to say things in a different manner, then in time the grammatical rules also change to reflect this. After all, languages are not static and the same language has had different grammatical rules at different time periods.

The same can be said for alphabetic writing systems. They are supposed to reflect the manner in which people speak. If the manner in which people speak changes over time, then so should the spelling system. This is a strong argument in favor of spelling reform.

Finally, in the same vein that it would make it easier for both children in English-speaking countries to learn to read, and for speakers of foreign languages to learn English, it would also help to reduce adult illiteracy in English-speaking countries.

1.6.3.2. The Negatives of Spelling Reform

After having discussed the advantages of spelling reform, it is now necessary to discuss the disadvantages. It is important to remember that some of these disadvantages are actually just obstacles that can be overcome without huge amounts of effort.

First of all, there is an obvious disadvantage: spelling reform would require everyone to learn a new system. This is especially true with an attempt to reform English, as there would be so many necessary changes, i.e. unlike in other languages where the overall percentage of words affected would be small, in English a large number of words would end up with a new spelling. Moreover, there is also the issue of the fact that so many books have already been written. It's unlikely that libraries would change their entire collections so that all of their books would be based on the new spelling. The same could be said about building inscriptions.

One interesting disadvantage to mention is the fact that by keeping the old spelling, we can read texts from centuries ago. Had English undergone spelling reforms several hundred years ago, as was suggested, texts from the High Middle Ages and the Early Modern Era would be incomprehensible to people today. By reforming spelling, that link could be severed.

Another disadvantage would be that the etymology of words would become less obvious. This is especially true of words of foreign origin. For example, the reason that the word "chef" is spelled with a "ch" rather than say, an "sh" is because the word is of French origin. If it were to be spelled say "shef", that origin would be less obvious. However, English is not the only language to have adopted a number of words of French origin. Both Swedish and Turkish have adopted a number of French words. In these two languages—even though they are both written with the same Latin alphabet as French—these French words have been given new spellings to match the respective Swedish and Turkish orthographies. For example, the Swedish word for "environment" comes from the French "milieu". However, in Swedish it is spelled "miljö". In the case of Turkish, the word for "restaurant bill" comes from the French "addition". However, in Turkish it is spelled "adisiyon". It would therefore not be a problem from English to give words from foreign languages a new spelling based on English orthography, a new and improved English orthography that is.

Furthermore, it is important to realize that some words would actually end up with a more cumbersome spelling. A good example of this is the word "fusion". Under a more phonetical orthography, this word might be written something like "fyoozhun". After all, the current spelling seems to indicate that a word spelled like that should be pronounced as either "fuss-i-on" or "fuss-ee-on". A more common word is "nation". A more phonetical spelling of "nation" would probably look more like "nayshun". After all, the current spelling indicates a word that should be pronounced like "na-tee-on". However, such cases will be uncommon and, in the end, it will not take long to become accustomed to this new spelling.

In addition, it could complicate grammatical endings. A good example of this is the addition of "ed" at the end of verbs in order to form the simple past/the past participle. In some verbs, such as "help" and "work", the addition of "ed" simply adds a "d" sound (or in some cases, more of a "t") and not an "ed" sound. By contrast, other verbs, such as "wait", have more of an "ed" (or even "et") sound in the past. All of these verbs add the same "ed" ending. If the reformed spelling were to become truly phonetical, then the new spelling of some these verbs in the past would have to be with an extra "ed" added at the end, whereas others would merely add a "d". There would even by the issue of the voiced "d" and "ed" versus voiceless "t" and "d". Likewise, the extra "s" in the third person singular could be affected by whether the first letter of the following word begins with a vowel. However, it is important to remember that this is already the case in English with regards to the two different indefinite articles, i.e. "a" versus "an". This would therefore not be a major obstacle. Likewise, it is not difficult to predict when to use a "d" versus a "t", etc. The same could be said about the plural of nouns with regards to an "s" versus a "z".

Another disadvantage to spelling reform is that it will no longer be possible to visually distinguish between homonyms. There are two notable examples of this within English clichés. For example, when an idea is seen as being incredibly stupid, it is often called "hare brained", the reason being that hares have small brains. However, as if often the case with clichés, their meanings become lost over time as people merely repeat them without having any clue as to their origin. Indeed, many clichés seem silly in their meaning, such as "chip on shoulder". As a result, people do not think it strange to repeat a cliché with a seemingly strange meaning. As a result of this, some people mistakenly think that "hare brained" is actually "hair brained". If spelling reform were to be implemented, "hare" and "hair" would have the same spelling.

Another example of this is the cliché, "toe the line". The meaning of this is being forced to support the official position, of say a political party. In this sense, "toe the line" means standing on the official line in a show of support. Some people mistakenly think that it is "tow the line" as in a towboat pulling a line, as in a metal cable. Such an expression probably would make sense as well, but that is not what the cliché is. Under spelling reform, "toe" and "tow" would have the same spelling. However, we should be reducing our use of clichés anyway. This would therefore not be a major issue.

Moreover, it is important to remember that there are plenty of words in English—along with other languages—that have the same spelling but mean completely different things. A great example of this is the word "spring". "Spring" can be a noun referring to a season of the year, a pool of water, a coil of metal, or a verb meaning to bounce. However, the verb is probably etymologically connected with the noun meaning "coil of metal". These three completely different nouns all have the same pronunciation and the same spelling. It would therefore not be a problem if words like "hair" and "hare" and "toe" "tow" ended up with the same spelling.

It is worth noting that English is not the only language in which this phenomenon can be found. For example, in Swedish, "gång" can refer to either an aisle or a time (i.e. three times, four times). In Albanian "verë" can mean either "summer" or "wine". One final example, in Ossetian "хид" can refer to either "bridge" or "sweat". However, it is also worth noting that in the Swedish example, these two nouns have different plurals. "Gång" when it means "time" adds an "er" in the plural, but when it means "aisle", it adds an "ar" in the plural.

An important issue, and this is especially true for English, would be what standard to use. This is particularly true when one considers that English is the main language in a number of different countries, such as the United Kingdom, the United States of America, Australia, Canada, and New Zealand. It is even more countries when one considers the fact that English is also the dominate or at least official language in so many other countries with which we are not so quick to associate it, countries such as India, Kenya, Nigeria, and Guyana. Some words are pronounced differently in these different countries.

Indeed, even within the same country, such as the United States, different words are sometimes pronounced differently. A good example of this is New England, where the "ar" is often pronounced without the "r" sound. The classic joke in Boston is that "park the car at Harvard Yard" is often pronounced "pak the ca at Havad Yad". Another good example is that New Jersey is often pronounced "New Joysey" in New Jersey. One final example, in eastern Virginia if a word ends with an "s" sound, a "t" sound is often added at the end. For example, the word "novice" is often pronounced as "novist" and the word "pace" is often pronounced as "pacet".

However, this is a minor consideration when one considers the fact that standard spellings are always based on a standard form of the language and do not take into consideration regional variations. In the case of English though, this may be a little more difficult when one considers the fact that the language is spoken in so many different countries. This study will be focusing on American English. However, it is likely that the proposals would be mostly effective in other English-speaking countries as well. Also, it is not a problem if some words are spelled differently in different English-speaking countries. After all, this is already the case. The most obvious example of this, as was previously mentioned, is the extra "u" in British English in a lot of the words ending in "or" in America English. A good example of this is the word "color", which is written as "colour" in Britain. It is therefore not a problem if some words are spelled differently in say, the United States versus Britain due to differences in the pronunciation of certain words in the two different English-speaking countries. Indeed, this would be a great way to highlight any differences between British and American English.

One interesting consideration is the fact that acronyms would change. For example, in boxing there is the acronym "KO". It comes from "knock out". However, any spelling reform of English would almost certainly drop the silent "k", meaning that "KO" would no longer be a logical acronym for "knock out". However, this would obviously be a very minor consideration, as such acronyms could either be changed or simply kept as they are, much as set expressions often are. For example, Bulgarian is one of the few Slavic languages to not have a regular case system, only remnants of an older case system. However, certain fixed expressions in Bulgarian are inflected properly based on a now non-existent case system. A good example of this is "Oh God", which in Bulgarian is "О Боже". The Bulgarian word for "God" is "Бог". "О Боже" is therefore "Бог" being properly inflected based on a case system that Bulgarian no longer has. Therefore, the issue about how it would affect acronyms need not be a concern. Besides, acronyms are overused anyway.

In a related issue, it is also worth noting that spelling reform could see a huge re-ordering with regards to alphabetical order. This is, of course, a very minor point and would not be of great significance. It is, however, worth mentioning.

There is also the issue of proper names, both place names and personal names. As for place names it is obvious: when necessary they will get a new spelling based on the new orthography. For example, the British city of Brighton would become, "Briiton", or whatever the new way of spelling the long "i" would be. Place names of foreign origin in English-speaking countries probably should retain their own foreign-based spellings. For example, in the US state of Wisconsin there is the city of "Eau Claire", meaning "clearwater" in French. Since it is of French origin, it need not be changed to "O Kler", or whatever the new orthography would indicate the new spelling for the sounds in question should be. In the case of place names in English-speaking countries that are based on indigenous languages, such as is often the case in countries such as the United States, Australia, and New Zealand, these place names should probably just retain their current spellings, even though, in most cases, they were partially based on present-day English orthography. Good examples of this include the US states of Tennessee and Kentucky. In the case of place names in Celtic parts of the British Isles, namely Ireland, Scotland, and Wales, if the spelling is based on the orthography of the Celtic language in question, obviously it should be retained. However, if it is based on present-day English orthography, then they should either change to reflect the new spelling in English or better yet, revert to the proper Celtic-based spelling.

The situation is a bit more difficult for surnames. The first issue to address is people living in English-speaking countries who have non-English surnames. The number is indeed huge since many of these countries, such as the United States, Canada, and Australia, became popular immigration destinations for people from outside the British Isles. Oftentimes, especially in the past, these names were changed to make it easier for English speakers. However, in the case of names that were not changed, they definitely should retain their current spellings. After all, a spelling reform in English should not affect their spellings since they were not based on English in the first place. As for those that were already adjusted to be made easier for English speakers, it would be up to the individuals with those names to decide whether they wish to change the spelling. This brings up what would be an important point should there be any change in the manner in which English is written: when in doubt, the default position is to retain the old spelling.

This brings up the issue of English last names which could change based on spelling. A good example of this would be the last name "Wright". Should people with this surname change the spelling to "Riit" or whatever the new English orthography says that three-sound combination should be spelled? In the end, it would of course be up to the individuals with those names to decide. However, a system must be put in place for people who wish to adapt their surnames to the new spelling easily do so.

It is worth noting that oftentimes people in the parts of Scotland where Scottish Gaelic is dominate will often spell their names in both the traditional Gaelic manner and the English manner, depending on the language in which they are writing at the time. A good example of this is my mother's own maiden name "Duncan". The traditional Scottish Gaelic spelling is "MacDhònnachaidh. It is therefore possible to have a system in place that, depending on the context, can regonize two different spellings for the same surname.

One final consideration is how it would affect our use of technology, as it is programmed based on the currently spelling system. However, this is a minor consideration as technology is being constantly updated.

Conclusions to Chapter 3

As is often the case in life, there are advantages and disadvantages. Spelling reform is no different, as there are a number of advantages and disadvantages to it.

The biggest advantage is an obvious one: the orthographic system in English would finally reflect the manner in which the words are spoken. It would be easy for people—both native speakers and those for whom English is a second language—to know exactly how to spell the words, as one would merely need to sound it out. This would also help English-speaking children learn to read, and would facilitate the learning of English for speakers of other languages. It would also help reduce adult illiteracy in English-speaking countries. There is even reason to believe that the rates of dyslexia in English-speaking countries would be reduced.

However, there are also disadvantages. First of all, there is the obvious: everyone would have to learn a new system. Also, the many books that have already been printed—not to mention things such as building inscriptions—will not be reprinted, at least not quickly. Also, computers would have to be reprogrammed. There are also other issues, such as no longer being able to visually distinguish between homonyms and a possible loss of the etymological origin of words.

In the end though, the advantages outweigh the disadvantages. Basically, the only real disadvantage is the effort in making the reform itself.

CHAPTER 4. SUGGESTED NEW WAY OF SPELLING THE ENGLISH LANGUAGE

Introduction to Chapter 4

Now, after having reviewed all the necessary background information: i.e. the history of the English language, how societies choose their orthographic systems, examples of spelling reforms in other languages (including outright changes in writing systems), and finally the pros and cons of spelling reform, it is now possible to consider what an actual orthographic reform in English would look like. As has been previously stated, this proposed spelling reform will use the Latin alphabet, rather than an alternative alphabet or non-alphabetic writing system. It will certainly not create a new writing system. Likewise, this particular study is based off of American English, though its suggestions would almost certainly be effective, at least mostly so, for the other English-speaking countries.

1.7.4.1. Diacritics

The first question is whether to use diacritics. Most of the other European languages written with the Latin alphabet include letters with diacritics. Indeed, it is strange that of all the European languages written in the Latin alphabet, it would be English that hardly ever uses diacritics, when it is English that has more sounds than most. There are, however, a small handful of words in English that are supposed to be written using diacritics. These words include "naïve", "naïveté", and "cliché". Interestingly, while typing these words, it was unnecessary to insert these diacritics under "symbols", as the autocorrect adds them automatically. Finally, it is important to remember that in Shakespeare's time, the "ed" added to the end of verbs to indicate the simple past was often written as "èd":

> Iago: Ay, there's the point: as, to be bold with you, Not to affect many proposèd matches (Shakespeare, 1968, p. 112)

Diacritics are found in a number of European languages using the Latin alphabet. There are a number of different diacritics which are used and there are several different reasons for using them:

Many languages supplement the basic Latin alphabet with a variety of accented letters:

Á á acute	È è grave	Î î circumflex	Õ õ tilde	Ů ů ring	Ÿ ÿ umlaut / diaeresis
Ą ą ogonek	Ě ě caron	Ī ī macron	Ơ ơ horn	Ŭ ŭ breve	Y y hook
Â â inverted breve	E̋ e̋ double grave	İ i dot above	Ø ø slash	Ű ű double acute	Ẏ ẏ dot below
Ç ç cedilla	Đ đ bar	Ł ł middle dot	Ỏ ỏ hook above	Ŧ ŧ slash	đ đ top bar

These accented letters can have a number of different functions:

- Modifying the pronunciation of a letter
- Indicating where the stress should fall in a word
- Indicating emphasis in a sentence
- Indicating pitch or intonation of a word or syllable

- Indicating vowel length
- Visually distinguishing homophones (Omniglot, 2019).

This also brings up an interesting possibility: should letters that once existed in English be revived? Indeed, these letters have a historical claim to being a part of English orthography: As strange as it sounds, the English alphabet had several more letters in the past few hundred years than it does today. Six more to be exact, including Ethel and Yogh (yup, those were the real names for "oi" sound, like in "coin," and "kh" sound like in "Loch Ness Monster" respectively). Linguistics experts say that modern streamlining and the mixing of the cultures of Northern Europe are to blame for their loss.

"Some former letters had significance, as Eth and Ash are still used as part of the phonemic chart used for pronunciation," says ESL professor Alix Hoechster, "but don't expect to see them on your keyboard or use them in day-to-day life." That's because they've generally been phased out and replaced by letters that do double duty, either by already addressing the sounds in question or by making the desired sounds when combined with other standard, existing letters (Gruber, 2019).

So basically, the six letters that once existed are:

Eth (ð)

The *y* in *ye* actually comes from the letter eth, which slowly merged with *y* over time. In its purest form, eth was pronounced like the *th* sound in words like *th*is, *th*at, or *th*e. Linguistically, *ye* is meant to sound the same as *the* but the incorrect spelling and rampant mispronunciation live on.

Thorn (þ)

Thorn is in many ways the counterpart to eth. Thorn is also pronounced with a *th* sound, but it has a voiceless pronunciation—your vocal cords don't vibrate when pronouncing the sound—like in *th*ing or *th*ought...

Wynn (ƿ)

Wynn was incorporated into our alphabet to represent today's *w* sound. Previously, scribes used two *u* characters next to each other, but preferred one character instead and chose wynn from the runic alphabet...

Yogh (ȝ)

Yogh was historically used to denote throaty sounds like those in *Bach* or the Scottish *loch*. As English evolved, yogh was quickly abandoned in favor of the *gh* combo. Today, the sound is fairly rare...

Ash (æ)

Ash is still a functional letter in languages like Icelandic and Danish. In its original Latin, it denoted a certain type of long vowel sound, like the *i* in *fine*. In Old English, it represented a short vowel sound—somewhere between *a* and *e*, like in *cat*. In modern English, æ is occasionally used stylistically, like in archæology or medæval, but denotes the same sound as the letter *e*.

Ethel (œ)

Ethel also once represented a specific pronunciation somewhere between the two vowels *o* and *e*, though it was originally pronounced like the *oi* in *coil*. Like many clarifying distinctions, this letter also disappeared in favor of a simpler vowel lineup (a, e, i, o, u) with many different pronunciations (Poindexter, 2017).

Some of these letters are currently used in other languages, such as the thorn in Icelandic. As to whether these letters should be revived will be considered later when the topic of the sounds which they could be used to represent comes up.

This brings up what is probably the most important decision to make with regards to spelling reform: is it best to start with the current orthography and change it, or is better to just start from the beginning and assign a different spelling to each sound? This research is going to be conducted based on the premise that it is better to have one exact way to spell each sound. Likewise, each sound should be spelled with one letter, with diacritics if necessary. In addition, one fixed two-letter combination should exist for all letters with diacritics as an alternative to using diacritics. However, the current system will be taken into consideration throughout the process. Also, some of these points may not work with each sound.

This just leaves one final issue for consideration: should the new English orthography show upon which syllable the stress should fall? Some other European languages written with the Latin alphabet, such as Spanish, do this. One of the reasons that Spanish does this is because the rules of stress are quite regular and these accent marks are used to show places where the stress does not follow the set pattern:

    A. "In Spanish, if a word has a written accent mark (called in Spanish **acento**), the accented syllable is stressed.

din__á__mico ri__dí__culo veinti__trés__

B. In words without a written accent, the following rules apply.

1. The next to last syllable is stressed if the word ends in a vowel, diphthong, or in **n** or **s**.

   __pa__tio re__pi__tan __lu__nes

2. The last syllable is stressed if the word ends in a consonant other than **n** or **s**.

   an__imal__ doc__tor__ liber__tad__" (Dawson, 1997, p. 5).

Greek, which does not use the Latin alphabet but instead has its own, places accent marks in all (or at least nearly all) multisyllabic words. The reason is the opposite of Spanish: the stress system in Greek is quite unpredictable: "From the above words and phrases you will have noticed the use of the stress-accent. With a few exceptions, it is used on every word with more than one syllable, and nowadays simply has the function of telling the reader which syllable must be stressed" (Watts, 2004, p. 5).

Indeed, prior to the Greek spelling reform mentioned in chapter two, it was quite common for a word in Greek to have several different stress marks. In fact, there were even diacritics to show breathing.

Interestingly, there are a number of English words that are written the same, but are pronounced differently and mean different things, with the difference in pronunciation being merely based on the stress falling on different syllables. A good example of this is the difference between the adjective "content"—where the stress falls on the second syllable—and the noun "content", where the stress falls on the first syllable. Here is a good sample sentence: the audience was content with the content. If a new orthographic system does not show syllable stress, these two words would continue to have the same spelling. Indeed, it is unlikely that spelling reform would affect these two words, other than to maybe change the "c" into a "k". In the end, it is actually not necessary to show stress marks.

If it is decided that stress should be shown, then it should be shown using an acute accent, like this: "é". If this research decides that there should be diacritics placed on vowels, such as "ā" to distinguish between a long "a" and a short "a", this would raise the issue of whether an accent mark could be added to "ā" to show that the stress falls on a syllable with a long "a" sound. If that were to happen, then software would have to be reprogrammed to create such a letter, as one is not there as of now. Interestingly, some letters with double diacritics are already available, such as "ā̈". However, it is unlikely that this proposed reform would use such a letter. Instead, this paragraph has already suggested a manner in which to do that and it is therefore obvious how words would look if this factor were to be taken into consideration.

In the end, this research will propose two possible spelling systems: one with diacritics and one without. Each of these two will have an exact match. For example, the [ʃ] sound can be spelled either with a "sh" (as is usually currently the case in English) or a "š", as it is spelled in many of the Central European Languages, such as Czech and Croatian. Therefore, the proposed new spellings of the word "chef" would be both "shef" and "šef". Generally speaking, it would probably be best to be consistent in the use (or non-use) of diacritics. For example, if the word "nation" becomes spelled "nayshun" without diacritics but as "nāšun" with diacritics, the spellings of "nāshun" and "nayšun" should not be used. In the same sense, the same essay should not use the new non-diacritic spellings on some words and the new diacritic spellings on others. This is based on the same thinking that writers should not mix British and American spellings.

It is worth noting that the three letters in the Swedish alphabet have diacritics— "å", "ä", and "ö" —have an exact equivalent without diacritics: "aa", "ae", and "oe", respectively.

At this point, it is necessary to review the different diacritics that other European languages written in the Latin alphabet use. The reason for this is to see which ones would be useful for a reformed English orthography. In each case examples are mentioned. The examples used hardly constitute an exhausted list.

The most common type of diacritic is the accent. The accent mark can go in either direction, i.e. either "é", which is known as "acute", or "è", which is known as "grave". Usually these accent marks are used to indicate things such as stress or length of the vowel. In some languages—such as Spanish and Irish Gaelic—the accent mark is always acute, i.e. "é", whereas in the case of Italian and Scottish Gaelic, it is always grave, i.e. "è". In the case of French, both are found. While this particular diacritic is usually only found on vowels, there are some instances—notably in Polish and Croatian—where it can be found on consonants as well. Examples of this include "ś" in Polish and "ć" in both Polish and Croatian.

These two letters are designed to spell sounds similar (though not identical) to the [ʃ] and [tʃ] sounds, respectively. In some languages, such as English and Swedish, this particular diacritic does not exist except in a handful of words of foreign—often French—origin. In addition, Hungarian also has a double acute accent on the "o" ("ő") and "u" ("ű"). Again, it is for the purpose of modifying vowel sounds.

The second most common diacritic in European languages is probably the umlaut. This diacritic is found in Swedish, German, French, Spanish, and Turkish, to mention a few. The umlaut is found over vowels and renders such letters as "ä", "ë", "ï", "ö", and "ü". In the case of Swedish, German, and Turkish, it is used to render a different vowel sound. In the case of French and Spanish, it is used to indicate that two vowels that are usually read together should be read separately.

Similar to the umlaut is the single dot over a vowel. In the case of Lithuanian, it is over the vowel "e", written as "ė". Again, this is to show a separate vowel sound. In the case of Maltese, it is written over the consonants "c", "g", and "z" as "ċ", "ġ", and "ż". In doing so, these consonants become pronounced as [tʃ], [dʒ], and [z], respectively. In the case of Maltese, the "z" without a dot is used to spell the [ts] sound rather than the [z].

There are two other notable examples of dots. In the case of Catalan, there is a raised dot between two "l"s: "L·l" as a capital letter, and "l·l" as a lowercase letter. This spells the sound [l:]. Interestingly, the Serbian variant of Cyrillic has a single letter for this: "љ". Another example is Turkish, where the "i" sometimes has a dot, and sometimes does not. This is true for both capital letters— "I" and "İ"—and lowercase letters, "ı" and "i". These show two different vowel sounds: [i] with a dot, and [ɯ] without a dot.

Another common diacritic is the tilde. This mark is found in Spanish and Portuguese. In the case of Spanish, it is found over the "n", as in "ñ", and it changes the "n" into a [ɲ] sound. In the case of Portuguese, it is used to change the pronunciation of the vowels "a" and "o", to make it more nasal, written as "ã" and "õ" respectively.

The use of the ring is not all that common outside of Scandinavia. Indeed, the only notable European language outside of Scandinavia to use the ring is Czech. Indeed, it is not even used in Slovak. In the case of the Scandinavian languages, it is over the "a", as "å". In the case of Czech, it is over the "u" as "ů". In both cases, it creates a different vowel sound.

The circumflex is used in some of the Romance languages, notably French, Portuguese, and Romanian. In all three cases, it modifies the pitch of the vowel sound in question.

Although unheard of in Western Europe, the caron is a commonly used diacritic in much of Eastern Europe, notably in languages such as Czech, Slovak, Slovene, and Croatian. In the case of Czech, for example, it appears on eight different letters, seven of which are consonants. The most common usage is to show different consonant sounds that are not available in the Latin alphabet. For example, "č" shows the [tʃ] sound and "š" shows the [ʃ] sound. This diacritic will probably prove to be quite useful.

One diacritic that is not all that common in European languages today, but that will probably prove to be quite useful, is the macron. Indeed, probably the only notable European language to use the macron is Latvian. In Latvian, the macron is used over certain vowels. Indeed, Latvian uses this diacritic over all vowels except "o". The purpose is to render different vowel sounds. For example, the "u" is pronounced as [u], whereas the "ū" is pronounced as [uː]. However, this diacritic is also colloquially used in English to distinguish between long and short vowels. It will therefore be a common diacritic in this proposal.

Another diacritic that is not particularly common amongst European languages is the breve. One notable example is Romanian, where it is used on the "a" as "ă", and is used to indicate the schwa [ə] sound. Another example is Turkish and Azeri, where the breve over a "g" ("ğ") is used to indicate a glottal stop for the preceding vowel.

The cedilla is one diacritic that makes different sounds in different languages. For example, in French and Portuguese, a cedilla on a "c" ("ç") ensures that the "c" will make a [s] sound. By contrast, in Albanian and Turkish it makes the [tʃ] sound. The cedilla is also used on the "s" in Romanian, making the [ʃ] sound. One final note on the cedilla: in Latvian there is a "g" with a cedilla. With a capital "G", it is as one would expect: "Ģ". However, with the lowercase it is written above the letter, as "ġ".

The slash is a really interesting diacritic. The reason it is interesting is because, first of all, it can be written in two different ways: either diagonally or horizontally. In the case of diagonally, there are two notable examples: the "ø" in

Danish and Norwegian, and the "ł" in Polish. In the case of Danish and Norwegian, it makes a distinct vowel sound. In the case of Polish, it makes a consonant sound that is somewhere between an "l" and "w".

The horizontal slash mark is found on several different letters in several different languages. A good example is the "Đ". This letter is found in both Icelandic and Croatian. However, this letter spells a completely different sound in each: [ð] in Icelandic and a variant of the English "j" in Croatian. Also, interestingly, while the capital letter is the same in both languages, the lower case on is not: it's "ð" in Icelandic, and "đ" in Croatian. Maltese also as a horizontal slash on the "h", "Ħ" as a capital and "ħ" as a lowercase letter. As is the case in neighboring Italian (even though it is from a completely different language family) the "h" is silent. By adding the slash, it becomes an "h" as in English. One final letter with a slash worth mentioning is the "ŧ". In some Sami dialects, this is used to spell the [θ] sound. This could prove useful in any attempt to reform English orthography.

The ogonek is not a common diacritic in many European languages. The two most notable examples of it are Polish and Lithuanian. This is one diacritic that is limited primarily to vowels. Again, it is used to show different vowel sounds. Even though showing different vowel sounds is an important part of any reform of English spelling, it is unlikely that this diacritic will be used.

Although the apostrophe is thought of more as being a punctuation mark—indeed, that is its primary function—in some languages, it is also used as a diacritic. It is therefore necessary to mention it here. One example of the apostrophe as a diacritic is Italian, where the lowercase "è" is often written as E' when written with a capital letter. Another example of this phenomenon is the "t" with a caron as a capital letter (such as in Slovak) is often written as a "t" with and apostrophe as a lowercase letter. Also in the case of Slovak, there is an "l" with an apostrophe. Unlike with the previous examples, in this case, the apostrophe is used with both the capital and lowercase letters.

There is one final mark to mention with regards to diacritics: ligatures. Ligatures are two letters written together. In some cases, they are thought of as being a single letter and are alphabetized as so. Some examples of this include the "ij" in Dutch, the "lj" in Slovene, and the "ll" and the "ch" in Spanish. However, ligatures are more often thought of as being two letters physically written together. The best examples of this are the "æ" in Danish and Norwegian and the "œ" in French. As was previously mentioned, both of these letters once existed in English and will be considered in this study. One final thing to mention with regards to ligatures, the German s-set: "ß". This represents two "s"s together and is written as such in Switzerland. This will probably prove to be of little use to a reformed spelling of English. It is worth noting though, that several hundred years ago in English there was a "long s" that looked like "ſ". Again, this will probably not be useful to this proposed reform, even though this letter once existed in English.

1.8.4.2. The Actual Proposal

After having reviewed everything, it is now possible to suggest an actual reformed way of spelling the English language. The first decision to make is whether to base it off of the old system, or whether to start over again with a sound to letter correlation. The decision here is that it would be better to have a sound for letter correlation, regardless of how different the new orthography would resemble the old one. Indeed, this could be a good way of distinguishing the current system from the new one. This will include words of foreign origin, meaning that they will not retain their foreign spellings. There is, after all, precedent for this. For example, Swedish, Albanian, and Turkish have adopted words of foreign origin, such as French, and given them new spellings based on their system of orthography. This is in spite of the fact that all of the languages in question use the Latin alphabet. It must be emphasized that this will not apply to people's names of foreign origin. For example, US citizens with a French last name would continue to use the French spelling of their surnames. It is worth noting that sometimes in Albanian, non-Albanian surnames will be transcribed into Albanian orthography, even if the person's name is from a language which also uses the Latin alphabet.

However, at the same time, the current system will still be used as a base for deciding the new system of spelling. For example, English is one of the few European languages (Catalan is another notable example) using the Latin alphabet where the letter "j" is pronounced as [dʒ]. In most cases, it is pronounced as [j]. In this proposed reform, the letter "j" will continue to be used to spell the [dʒ] sound. Indeed, this proposed reform will use the letter "j" to spell the [dʒ] sound, even in instances where the letter "g" is currently used, like in the word "giraffe".

The second big issue is whether to use diacritics. Such marks were discussed in depth in the previous sub-chapter. This proposed reform will suggest both: i.e. one system with diacritics, and one system without. For example, the [ʃ] sound should always be spelled the same way. Presently, it is spelled differently in the words "short" "chef", "sure", and "nation". Under this proposed reform, this sound will always be spelled one way without diacritics as "sh", and one way with diacritics "š". As a result, these words will now be spelled as either "short" or "šort", "shef" or "šef", "shur" or "šur", and "nayshun" or "nāšun".

Having reviewed everything, it is now possible to take each sound in English and assign a single letter to it, or a fixed two-letter combination with a single letter with a diacritic as a substitute.

4.2.1. Consonant Sounds

It is probably best to begin with the consonant sounds. There are several reasons for this. First of all, the problems with English spelling stem more from the vowel sounds. There is therefore less reform needed with regards to the consonants. Also, there are more consonant sounds than vowel sounds. Indeed, there are approximately 24 consonant sounds versus 15 or so vowel sounds, depending on such factors as how one distinguishes between different sounds and the different parts of the English-speaking world in question. At the same time, there are 20 consonants and 5 vowels, with "y" going both ways. There are therefore many more consonants than vowels available, even though there are only slightly more consonant sounds than vowel sounds. Moreover, the reforms of consonant sounds are much more straightforward. Indeed, the majority of consonant sounds will require zero reform. As a result, many consonant sounds (such as [b]) will not even be mentioned, as they will see no changes under this proposed reform.

Before getting into the sound for sound analysis of spelling reform for each consonant sound in English, it is best to start with obvious reforms. First of all, all silent consonants should be dropped. Examples of this include the silent "k" in "kn" combinations (such as "knee", which should become "nee", or "nē"), and the silent "w", in "wr" combinations (such as "wren", which should now be "ren"). It is worth noting that there are silent vowels as well, such as the "u" in "build". Obviously, these silent vowels will be dropped as well, and "build" will become "bild".

One consonant that is always silent is the "h" in "wh" words, such as "when". These days, there is no difference in pronunciation between "w" (as in "water") and "wh" (as in "when"). In modern Swedish, there is the [ɧ] sound. There are a number of different ways that this sound is spelled in Swedish, but "sj" is probably the most common. It is likely that the "wh" was meant to spell this sound. However, since this sound no longer exists, there is no reason to write an "h" after a "w". Therefore, words such as "what" will now be "wat". It is important to note that not all Swedish speakers say this sound. Instead, they say [tʃ]. It is also important o note that there are words in Swedish (such as "tjur", meaning "bull") which are always pronounced as [tʃ] and never [ɦ].

Just as the "wh" is designed for a sound that no longer exists, so is the far less common "rh" (as in "rhetoric"). This spelling is also used in Welsh. In Welsh it spells the sounds [r̥]:

[Rh] is an aspirated 'r'—in practice it generally sounds as if it were written **hr**. (King, 1995, p. 4)

It is likely that the "rh" combination was used to spell the same sound in English. However, since that sound no longer exists, the "h" has become superfluous. The new spelling of "rhetoric" will now be "retorik".

Also, there is no need for double consonants. As a result, words such as "tell" should become "tel". In the same vein, there is no need for a "ck" combination anywhere. Instead, they should be spelled with a single "k". Therefore, words like "slick" should become "slik".

The example of the "ck" becoming a single "k" brings up the issue of how to spell the [k] sound in general. There is a surprising variety of ways in which this sound is spelled. The most common way in which this sound is spelled in English is with the letter "c" (as in "can"). However, a "c" before an "i" or "e" is pronounced as [s]. Therefore, in these situations the [k] sound is spelled with a "k", examples of this include "king" and "kettle". Likewise, words in English that end with that sound usually do not end with the letter "c". The previously mentioned example of "rhetoric" (which should now be spelled as "retorik"), however, is one example.

Instead, the word in question usually either ends with a "que" (as in "antique") or a single "k" (as in "junk"). In all these cases, this sound should be spelled with a simple "k". Therefore, the words "can" and "antique" will now be "kan" and "anteek" (or "antēk"), respectively.

In the same manner, the "qu" sound will now be spelled as "kw", so "queen" will now be "kween". The word "quick"—which has the [k] sound in two places—will now be "kwik". Indeed, it is not uncommon to see businesses in the United States with the word "kwik" in their names. Finally, the Middle Eastern country of "Iraq" will now be spelled as "Irak". In fact, Iraq is already spelled that way in a number of other languages, such as Swedish.

As a result of this, the letter "q" will no longer be necessary. This is the only letter that this proposed reform is definitely suggesting to eliminate, though there are several others that could also be eliminated. As was previously mentioned, there are six letters that used to exist in the English language. This proposal is suggesting that some of them be brought back (more on this later).

Just as the letter "c" will no longer be used to spell the [k] sound, it will also no longer be used to spell the [s] sound. Therefore, the word "cent" will now be "sent", which is already a word, meaning "the simple past of the verb 'to send'". The new spelling of "circle" will now be "surkul" (more on the change in the "le" ending later).

Based on the previous paragraphs, one could wonder whether the letter "c" will be eliminated altogether, much like the letter "q". However, there is still the issue of the [tʃ] sound, which in English is usually spelled as "ch" (as in "chain"). First of all, it is important to remember that the [tʃ] sound is not exclusively spelled as "ch". For example, this sound is spelled "tch" in "witch" and "t" in "nature". As is the case with all of the sounds in the English language, this proposal wants to foresee just one possible spelling per sound, or at the most two, with the second one having diacritics. In the case of the [tʃ] sound, however, there are several possible ways to suggest a uniform spelling. The first one is obvious: always spell this sound using a "ch" when not using diacritics, in which case "witch" and "nature" will now be "wich" and "naychur".

However, it is also possible to simply write a "c". After all, if the only time that the letter "c" is to remain in the English language is to spell the [tʃ] sound, then the use of the "h" in "ch" would become superfluous. Indeed, there is actually precedent for this, as this is how the [tʃ] sound is spelled in Malay and Indonesian. If that were to be the case, then the words "witch" and "nature" would become "wic" and "naycur", respectively.

One other possible way to spell this sound is with the letter "č". This is how this sound is spelled in languages such as Czech, Slovak, Slovene, and Croatian. Indeed, this diacritic will be suggested for the spelling of other sounds. The words "witch" and "nature" would become "wič" and "nāčur" (more on the new spelling of the long "a" later), respectively.

This is a difficult decision to make, as on the one hand there is any easy solution: the [tʃ] sound should always be spelled as "c", since that is a single letter with no diacritics. However, native English speakers are simply not accustomed to seeing a stand-alone "c" representing the [tʃ] sound. Instead, they would be likely to read the words "wic" and "naycur" (or "nācur"), as being "wik" and "naykur", respectively. However, it would not take long for people to become accustomed to this new spelling convention, and this would be the easiest way to spell the [tʃ] sound. After all, is not the point of this a simplification of spelling? There will therefore be no need to spell this sound with diacritics, and this proposed reform suggests that the "c" alone should always be used to spell the [tʃ] sound.

It is worth noting that the other European alphabets—with the exception of Greek, which does not even have this sound—all have a single letter for the [tʃ] sound. In the case of Cyrillic, it is usually "ч", though the Serbian variant also has the "ћ", as Serbian makes a slight distinction between the two sounds. The Georgian alphabet also has two different letters for two similar sounds, the "ჩ" and the "ჭ". The Armenian alphabet also has two different letters, the "չ" and the "ճ".

Another sound that if often needlessly complicatedly spelled is the [dʒ] sound. This is in spite of the fact that there is a single letter in the English language for this sound, the "j". However, this sound is sometimes spelled with a "g" (as in "gin") or, worse yet, as a "dg" (as in "edge" and "bridge"). The obvious solution is to spell these words as "jin", "ej", and "brij", respectively. The word "college" would see a spelling improvement in three places. First of all, the "c" would become a "k"; the double "l" would become a single "l"; and the "ge" would become a "j". The new spelling of "college" would therefore be a far better "kolej". A great example would be "hodgepodge", which will now be "hojpoj".

A very easy fix will be to change all "ph" spellings into "f" spellings. For example, "pharmacy" will now be "farmasee", or "farmasē" (more on the changes to vowel spellings later).

Unlike other European languages which use the Latin alphabet, English does not have a single letter for the [ʃ] sound. The most notable examples from other European languages include the "š" in Czech, Slovak, Slovene, Croatian, Latvian, and Lithuanian, and "ş" in Romanian and Turkish. Instead, the most common way to spell the [ʃ] sound in English is "sh". There are, however, some notable exceptions. First of all, the "ch" is sometimes used, especially in loan words from languages such as French. A good example of this is the word "chef". Also, the "t" in words such as "nation". Moreover, sometimes an "s" stands on its own, such as in "sure". Obviously, the best way to consistently spell the [ʃ] sound without diacritics will be with the "sh". Therefore, the words "chef", "nation", and "sure" will now be "shef", "nayshun", and "shur", respectively. The best way to spell this sound with diacritics is probably the most commonly used one: "š". With diacritics, these words will now be "šef", "nāšun", and "šur", respectively. It is worth noting that the other European alphabets—with the notable exception of Greek, which does not even have this sound—all have a single letter for this sound: "ш" in Cyrillic, "შ" in Georgian, and "շ" in Armenian. It is also worth noting that the Hebrew abjad has a single letter for this sound: "שׁ".

Another sound in need of a revised spelling is the voiced equivalent of the [ʃ], the [ʒ]. Again, the Latin alphabet does not in and of itself offer a single letter to spell this sound. Also again, there are European languages that have a letter with a diacritic to spell this sound. The most common one is the "ž", found in Czech and Slovak. In the case of Maltese, the "ż" is used. Interestingly, unlike the [ʃ] sound, the [ʒ] sound does not have as many equivalents in the other alphabets of Europe. Neither Greek nor most versions of Cyrillic (North Macedonian is an exception to this. They have the letter "s".) have this letter. In the case of Georgian, it is "ð", and in Armenian "d".

This is not one of the more common sounds in English. The few times it appears, it is usually written as a "g" (as in "garage") or as an "s" (as in "pleasure"). The most obvious way to consistently spell this sound without diacritics would be with a "zh". Indeed, this is already the way this sound is spelled in Albanian. Therefore, these two words will be "garazh" and "plezhur", respectively. The most obvious single letter with a diacritic to use for this sound is "ž". With diacritics, these two words will be "garaž" and "plezur", respectively.

Another sound that is spelled with two letters is the [ŋ], which is always spelled with an "ng". Unlike so many other examples in this study, this sound is not spelled any other way. There is therefore no need to suggest a fixed, two-letter spelling for this sound. That just leaves the issue of how to spell this sound with diacritics. Again, it is best to look to other European languages for the answer to this question. There are three different examples amongst the other

European languages, the "ň" in Czech, the "ñ" in Spanish, and the "ņ" in Latvian.

Before deciding which one to use, it must be remembered that there is a voiceless equivalent to this letter, which is spelled with an "nk". This is not often seen as being a separate sound. However, "sing" and "sink", and "ring" and "rink" are clearly separate words that are easily distinguished from each other when spoken. If a letter with a diacritic is going to be suggested for one, then so should there be a letter with a diacritic for the other. Of the three possibilities, there is no one obvious choice as to which of them to use, or which one to assign to which of the two sounds. In fact, there are even other logical possibilities. For example, there is the Latvian "ģ" (the capital letter equivalent is "Ģ") for the "ng", and the "ķ" for "nk". Other possibilities for the "ng" include the "ġ", which is found in Maltese, though it is used to spell a different sound, the [dʒ] sound, and the "ğ", which is used in Turkish to show a glottal stop.

The decision here is to use the "ñ" for the "ng" and the "ň" for the "nk". Again, there is no obvious way to assign these different letters to the two sounds in question. However, it must be noted that part of the reason the "ģ", "ğ", "ġ", and "ķ" were not chosen is that those letters are not used in their respective languages to spell the sounds in question. However, it must be emphasized that that is not a requirement for suggesting changes to English orthography. Therefore, the words "sing", "sink", "ring", and "rink" when written with diacritics will now be "siñ", "siň", "riñ", and "riň", respectively.

Interestingly, none of the other European alphabets has a single letter for this sound. However, it is interesting to note that the Runic alphabet had a single letter, "◊". That being said, one of the letters which used to exist in English was the "ŋ", which was for spelling this sound. Although this letter is not currently used anywhere in Europe except for some Sami languages, it is used in some African and Native American languages. It is therefore available on most computers. As a result, this study is also suggesting that this letter could also be revived and used to spell the "ng", but not the "nk" sound. In that case, the words "sing" and "ring" will become "siŋ" and "riŋ", respectively.

Another important consonant spelling issue to address is the "th". First of all, it must be stated that, while many native English speakers are not aware of this, this spelling is actually used to spell two—and not one—different sounds, [θ] and its voiced equivalent, [ð]. These two sounds are not all that common in the other European languages. Indeed, the only European alphabet to even have single letters to spell these sounds is Greek, where the [θ] is "θ" and the [ð] is "δ". Amongst the European languages that use the Latin alphabet, Albanian, Icelandic, and Welsh are three notable examples of languages that have these two sounds. In the case of all three of these languages, a distinction is made between these two different sounds, i.e. they are written differently. In the case of the [θ], both Albanian and Welsh used the "th" spelling, just like English. In the case of the [ð], Albanian uses "dh" and Welsh uses "dd".

Icelandic is an interesting case since they have preserved one of the old Runic letters to spell the [θ] sound, the "þ". Indeed, as was previously mentioned, this is one of the letters that English used to have, but no longer does. This brings up an exciting possibility: should this letter be brought back to English? The alternative would be to find a "t" with a diacritic. Presently, if one looks at other European languages using the Latin alphabet, one finds the "ț" in Romanian, the ť (the capital letter equivalent is "Ť") in Czech and Slovak, and the "ŧ" in Northern Sami. Interestingly, while the Romanian, and Czech and Slovak "t"s with diacritics are used to spell different sounds ([ts] in Romanian and [c] in Czech and Slovak), the ŧ is indeed used to spell the [θ].

This therefore brings up an interesting question: what is the best way to show the [θ] sound with a single letter in a reformed English spelling? First of all, the Romanian "ț" can immediately be dismissed as a possibility. After all, this proposed reform has preferred the caron diacritic over the cedilla. However, that then brings up the issue of whether to use the caron with the "t"—as has been the case with other letters such as "s" and "n" —or to use the Northern Sami "ŧ", which is actually used to spell the [θ] sound. At the same time, there is the possibility of using the Icelandic "þ", which actually used to be an English letter. In the end, this proposed reform is suggesting that the "þ" be returned to English, with the Northern Sami "ŧ" as an acceptable substitute. As a result, the word "thin" can continue to be spelled as "thin", or it can now be spelled as "þin" or "ŧin". Again, this proposal is not suggesting the spelling "ťin" ("Ťin" with the first letter being a capital letter) for the word "thin".

As was previously mentioned, the "th" is also used to spell the [ð] sound in English. Again, the only alphabet in

Europe to have a single letter to spell this sound is Greek, which has the "δ" ("Δ" as a capital letter). As of now, English makes no distinction orthographically between [θ] and [ð], as both as spelled with "th". This needs to change. Therefore, when written without diacritics, the [ð] should now be spelled as "dh". The word "them" will now be "dhem".

As for the best manner in which to spell the [ð] with just one letter, there is a similar situation as there is with the [θ] sound. Once again, there is a letter that once existed in English to spell this sound and still exists in Icelandic, the "ð" ("Ð" as a capital letter). Interestingly, the same capital letter, the "Ð", is used in Croatian to spell a sound similar to the [dʒ] sound. However, the lowercase letter looks differently, as it is written as "đ". It is worth noting that the Serbian Cyrillic equivalent of this letter is "ђ".

There is an available letter using the caron, ď ("Ď" as a capital letter). As was the case with the ť, this letter appears in both Czech and Slovak. As was also the case with Czech and Slovak, it is used to spell a different sound, the [ɟ], rather than the [ð] sound. Therefore, this reform suggests that the Icelandic "ð"—which once existed in English anyway—be revived and used again to spell the [ð] sound. As a result, "them" would now be spelled as "ðem" ("Ðem" with the first letter being a capital).

There is one final issue with regards to the "th" spelling: words in which the "th" is pronounced as [t] rather than [θ] or [ð]. In other words, words in which the "h" is in essence silent. A classic example of this is "Thomas rows on the Thames". This issue has an obvious fix: drop the "h": "Tomas rōz on ðu Tems".

One sound that English has in a few words but does not distinguish orthographically is [ʎ]. A few examples of this include the word "million", and the name "William". However, it is important to note that there are words in English, such as "pillow", with a double "l" which do not make this sound. Likewise, both of the above-mentioned examples include an "i" after the double "l". The Serbian variant of Cyrillic has a single letter for this sound: "љ". Catalan uses a double "l" with a raised dot between them: "l·l". In Slovak there is an "l" with an apostrophe. In Portuguese this sound is spelled with an "lh". It must also be remembered that in Spanish the double "l" tends to spell the [j]sound, though in some parts of the Spanish speaking world it is pronounced [dʒ] or [ʒ]. In the case of English, it would be best to spell this sound with a "ly" without diacritics, so "million" and "William" will become "milyun" and "Wilyam", respectively. Probably the best diacritic to use on the "l" is the slash mark, as in "ł". This letter is already used in Polish, though it spells a different sound in Polish. As a result, "million" and "William" would now with diacritics be "miłun" and "Wiłam", respectively.

The final consonant issue to address is whether to keep the letter "x". Many of those who have suggested spelling reform in the past have suggested that this letter be dropped. They believe that it serves no purpose. However, while it is possible to substitute the "x" with a "ks" in words such as "box", why write with two letters that which we can already write with one? After all, with regards to other sounds this proposal is suggesting that single letters, often with diacritics, be used. It would make no sense to drop a single letter that is already used. However, in instances where the "x" is used to spell the [z] sound (as in "xenophobia"), the "z" should replace the "x". This would therefore be "zeenifoabeea" without diacritics and "zēnifōbēa" with diacritics.

4.2.2. Vowel Sounds

The vowels will prove to be the trickiest part. This is not surprising given that a wide variety of vowel sounds is a noted characteristic of Germanic languages. German, Dutch, and Swedish, for example, also have a wide-range of vowel sounds. Likewise, although this study is primarily focused on American English, it is still important to remember that it is in the vowel sounds more than anywhere else that the differences between British and American English can most plainly be observed. Indeed, regional variations within British and American English can also often be seen in the differences in the vowel sounds: "Although there are only 5 vowel **letters** in English, there are actually 15 unique vowel **sounds**" (ESL Charts, 2019).

The actual number of vowel sounds varies depending on factors such as differences in regional pronunciation and how quick one is to consider a vowel sound as distinct, rather than just a variation of the same vowel sound. Anyway, the Latin alphabet only has 5 vowels, 6 if one considers the "y" as a vowel. A very cursory glance of simple arithmetic shows that it is not easy to spell 15 distinct sounds with only 5, maximum 6 different letters.

It is for this obvious reason—the lack of adequate vowels—that numerous two-vowel combinations have been used to spell vowel sounds in English. It is interesting to note the example of Dutch, a fellow Germanic language that also has numerous vowel sounds and needs to make a distinction between the long and short vowels: note that the long vowels are written double in closed syllables and single in open syllables, which is one of the basic rules of Dutch spelling (Donaldson, 1996).

However, in the case of English, there has been a lack of consistency with regards to how these two-vowel combinations have been used. Indeed, the introductory sentence: "I hear that you learned to create, break, and eat heart-shaped bread while watching reality television." had the "ea" combination eight different times, spelling eight different sounds. This is even true in the same written word, as "read" is pronounced "reed"—itself a word referring to a stick—in the present tense, and as "red"—itself a word referring to a color—in the past tense. What is therefore needed is a fixed, two-vowel combination—or better yet a vowel with a diacritic—to spell these different vowel sounds. In some instances, the Dutch example of merely writing the same vowel twice will prove useful.

At this point, it is necessary to consider a few guidelines on how to determine what two-letter vowel combinations should be created, and which diacritics to use. First of all, it must absolutely be emphasized that the time has long come to end the ridiculous practice of using a silent "e" at the end of the word to make the vowel long. While the word "hat" will not need a new spelling, the word "hate" will. The most logical new spelling of "hate" without diacritics would be either "hait" or "hayt". This study is recommending "hayt".

Prior to addressing which two-vowel combinations should be created and which diacritics should be used, it is necessary to begin with the sounds the single vowels make. This is the most obvious case. Each of the 5 vowels, "a", "e", "i", "o" and "u", have a recognized short sound. These vowels, when used on their own, will continue to show their respective short sounds. However, even in this case there will be some changes. For example, the "ea" in "heart" will become a short "a", "hart". The past tense of "read", will now be "red". The word "said", will now be "sed". The word "love" will now be "luv". The word "cough" will now be "kof". Finally, the word "enough" will now be "inuf".

The next step is to create a set, two-vowel combinations for the long vowel equivalents of these five vowels. However, before reviewing the long-vowel equivalents of these five letters, it is necessary to mention one other short-vowel: the [ʊ], often described as the "double oo" sound. This sound is found in words such as "good", "would" and "push".

This is probably the hardest sound with which to deal since there is no obvious suggestion to make. The most obvious example, a single "u", would not work as it would make no distinction between this sound and the short "u" sound [ʌ], as in "putt" and "touch". Indeed, the words "putt" and "put" would end up with the same spelling, since the double "t" in "putt" would be dropped, as there are to be no more double consonants.

The other obvious possibility—indeed, one that is already in use—would be to use a double "oo", as in "book". However, the obvious problem with this is that this spelling is also used to spell the long equivalent of this sound [u], as in "moon".

The best way to spell this sound without diacritics would be with the double "u". As a result, "good", "would", "push", and "put", will all become "guud", "wuud", "puush", and "puut", respectively. As for spelling this sound with diacritics, again, there is no obvious answer. While it would probably be best to add a diacritic to a "u", the question is: which one? The most logical one seems to be an acute accent: ú. Therefore, the words "good", "would", "push", and "put", will all become "gúd", "wúd", "púš", and "pút", respectively.

There is one final point with regards to the short vowels: the short "a". In American English, this sound is often pronounced as [æ]. In this case, it might make sense to spell this sound as "ä", as this is the manner in which this sound is spelled in Swedish, or as "æ", as it is in Danish and Norwegian. Indeed, the Danish/Norwegian spelling is a letter that used to exist in English. However, in the end this will prove to be superfluous, as there is no other sound that a standalone letter "a" will spell.

It is now possible to examine the best ways in which to spell the long vowel sounds. These six sounds will each be examined without diacritics at first, and then with diacritics.

There are basically two logical ways to spell a long "a" [eɪ], either "ai" (as in "pain") or "ay" (as in "say"). Theoretically either one would be equally logical. However, a choice must be made. The choice here is for the "ay". Therefore, "pain" is now "payn" and "say" remains the same. It is important to note that the Dutch example of double writing the vowel has no precedent—not that having a precedent is a requirement—in English with regards to the letter "a". It is for this reason that this study is not recommending the spellings of "paan" and "saa".

In the case of the long "e" [i], there is an obvious choice: write the letter "e" twice. This is already the case in numerous English words, such as "need" and "see". As a result, words such as "eat" and "either" will now be "eet" and "eethur" (more on the "ur" at the end of "either" later). It is worth noting that "even" will end up with a slightly more difficult spelling, as "eeven".

The long "i" [ɑɪ] at first glance appears to be the hardest one for which to create a two-vowel combination. After all, this sound is currently spelled in so many different ways, such as "i" with a silent "e" (as in "line") "igh" (as in "tight"), and "ind" (as in "kind"). In the end though, it is probably the easiest one, as the best thing to do is to simply use the Dutch example of the double letter. While there is no precedent for that in English (Indeed, skiing is probably one of the few times the "i" is written in double in English), it is the most logical change to suggest. Therefore, the words "line", "tight", and "kind" will now be "liin", "tiit", and "kiind", respectively. Interestingly, "kind" now has a longer spelling. However, thanks to this, it will finally be possible to visually distinguish between "wind" as in "blowing air" (this spelling will remain the same) and "wind" as in say "turning a mechanical clock", which will now be "wiind". It is worth noting that "sight", "site", and "cite" will all now have the same spelling: "siit".

In the case of the long "o" [oʊ], it will probably be best to retain the "oa" combination, as in "boat". Therefore "row the boat" will now be "roa the boat". This would, however, lead to longer spellings for the words "no" and "go", which would now be "noa" and "goa". "Know" would also now be "noa". The Dutch model of the double vowel would probably not be a good idea here, as the double "o" has historically been used in English to spell the long "oo" sound [u], as in "boot" (see the next paragraph).

Before discussing the long "u" [ju], it would be best to discuss the long "oo" sound [u]. In this case, it would be best to keep the double "oo", as in "moon". Other ways in which this sound is currently spelled include "ue" (as in "rue") and "u" with a silent "e" (as in "rude"). These words would now be "roo" and "rood", respectively.

As for the long "u" [ju], the most logical use under the current system is probably the double "o" with a "y" in front of it. This is therefore the only vowel sound (or indeed any sound) for which three rather than two letters will be necessary to spell a single sound without diacritics. Therefore, words such as "unique" will now be "yooneek". Likewise, "few" will now be "fyoo". This is one instance where the new spelling will look more complicated than the old.

After having created fixed, two-vowel combinations for these long vowel sounds, it is now necessary to create diacritics to show these long vowel sounds. The most obvious one to use is a macron over the vowel, like this: "ā". This mark has been used colloquially before, at least in the United States. Likewise, this mark is officially used in the Latvian language. It is therefore possible to show the long "a", "e", "i", "o", and "u", as "ā", "ē", "ī", "ō", and "ū", respectively.

Based on the current spelling system, the long "a" is spelled as "ai" (as in "pain"), "ay" (as in "say"), and a with a silent e (as in "hate"). As a result of this, the word "pain" is now "pān", "say" is now "sā", and "hate" is now "hāt". Another spelling of this sound is "ei" (as in "rein" and "weigh"). "Rein" will now be "rān", as would be "rain". Weigh will now be "wā", as will be "way". Likewise, "weight" will now be "wāt", as will be "wait".

The long "e" has numerous spellings. The most common are "ee", (as in "see") and "ea" (as in "eat"). These words will now be spelled as "sē" and "ēt", respectively. Other examples of how this sound is spelled include the "ei" (as in "neither") and "ie" (as in "piece"). Based on the new spelling system, "neither" will now be "nēður", and "piece" will now be "pēs", as will be "peace".

It is with the long "i" that the greatest improvement will be seen. After all, the cumbersome "igh" will be gone. The words "line", "tight", and "kind" are now "līn", "tīt", and "kīnd", respectively. Likewise, "sight", "site", and "cite" are all now "sīt". Finally, "wind" is now "wīnd" when it refers to "turning a clock" rather than "blowing air".

The long "o" sound will also be easy to improve, as it will now be spelled with a single "ō". Therefore, the words "row" and "boat" will now be "rō" and "bōt", respectively. Interestingly, the words "go" and "no" will still be the same length, though the "o" will now have a diacritic over it, now making these words "gō" and "nō", respectively. Likewise, "no" and "know" will now have the same spelling, as "nō".

The long u sound is one instance where the new spelling with diacritics will clearly be better than without, as "ū" is better than "yoo". It is, after all, better to spell "unique" and "few" as "ūnēk" and "fū", rather than "yooneek" and "fyoo".

In the case of the long "oo" [u] sound, the best thing would be a "u" with a circle, as in "ů". This letter is used in Czech to spell the same sound. The words "moon", "rue", and "rude", would all now be "mům", "rů", and "růd", respectively.

The next vowel sound to mention is the schwa [ə], often called the unstressed vowel. Interestingly, this is an actual letter in Azerbaijani. Indeed, this letter is used in the spelling of the name of the country itself: Azərbaycan. In the case of English, a simple "u" should be adequate for spelling this sound. Several examples of this have already been mentioned. Just above was the example of "either", which should now be "ēður". Indeed, the very word "above" should now be "ubuv".

The last three vowel sounds to mention are diphthongs: the [ɔɪ], [ɔ], and [aʊ] sounds.

The [ɔɪ] is usually spelled with either a "oy" (as in "boy"), or a "oi" (as in "foist"). For the sake of consistency, there should only be one of these spellings used when writing this sound. This research is suggesting—again for the sake of consistency—to use the "oy" rather than the "oi". After all, a similar decision was made with regards to the spelling of the long "a" sound without diacritics, i.e. "ay" and not "ai".

Therefore, "foist" will now be "foyst", whereas "boy" will remain "boy".

As for using diacritics to spell this sound, this is one instance where it is possible to revive a letter from the past. The "œ" was previously used to write this sound. This letter is currently used in French, albeit to spell a different sound. This proposal is calling for this letter to be returned to the English language. Therefore, the words "boy" and "foist" will now be "bœ" and "fœst", respectively.

The [ɔ] sound is almost always spelled with an "aw", as in "law". Since that is already one commonly recognized two-letter combination, there is no need to create a new one. There is also an obvious diacritic to use in this case, the circumflex. Therefore, "law" will now be spelled as "lâ" when spelled with a diacritic.

The last vowel sound to consider is the [aʊ] sound, usually either spelled with an "ou" (as in "sound" itself), or an "ow" (as in "cow"). As has been the case with several previous examples, both ways—i.e. "ou" and "ow"—make equal sense. However, for the want of consistency, one must be chosen. This proposal chooses to use the "ow" over the "ou". As a result, "sound" is now "sownd", whereas "cow" stays the same. As for diacritics, the best one to use would be an "o" with a breve: ŏ. As a result, "sound" is now "sônd" and "cow" is now "cŏ".

There is one final spelling issue to mention: the "le" ending in words such as "purple". This should be changed to "ul". Therefore, "purple" will now be "purpul".

1.9.4.3. Final Considerations

There are several final issues to mention. First of all, there is the issue of how set the spelling should be. Originally, this research was going to include an appendix listing all of the English words that would end up with a new spelling. However, for several reasons, this was not included. First of all, the whole point of this system is that it would be so easy, that the spelling of words under it would be so predictable that such an appendix would be redundant. Also, it is perhaps best not to be too strict at first with the new spellings, so that people can become more accustomed to them.

Moreover, with some words there could be some debate as to the best way to spell certain words. Indeed, the word "certain" itself is debatable. For starters, the "c" should be an "s". Both of the vowel sounds are unclear. Should the "e" become an "i" or "u"? Also, should the "ai" become a "u", an "i", or an "ā"? Again, it is best to not be so rigid at first. In the same manner, a "t" often becomes a "d" in American English when it appears in the middle of the word between two vowels. Should such "t"s now be written as "d"s?

The last issue is the new order of the letters. This is how it should be:

Aa Āā Ââ Bb Cc Dd Ðð Ee Ēē Ff Gg Hh Ii
Īī Jj Kk Ll Łł Mm Nn Ňň Ŋŋ (or Ññ) Oo Ōō
Ôô Œœ Pp Rr Ss Šš Tt Þþ (or Ŧŧ) Uu Ūū Ůů
Úú Vv Ww Xx Yy Zz Žž

As one can see, there will now be 42 letters, two of which have a possible substitution. Only the letter "q" was eliminated, while four letters that used to be in the alphabet in English are now back.

Conclusions to Chapter 4

After having reviewed all the necessary background information and weighed the advantages and disadvantages, it was finally possible to suggest an actual reformed manner in which to spell the English language.

The first question was whether to use diacritics. Nearly all of the other European languages written with the Latin alphabet use diacritics. It is strange that English—the one that probably has the most sounds—is the one that, with a small handful of exceptions, never uses diacritics. In the end, it was decided to use diacritics with a set two-letter (in one case three-letter) substitution for those who do not wish to use diacritics or are in situations where, for whatever reason, that would be difficult. The diacritics that are suggested are all already in existence and are, in nearly all cases, already used to spell the same sounds that this proposal is suggesting. In the same vein was the issue of whether to revive any of the letters which once existed in English. In the end, this proposal suggested bringing back several of these letters. In some cases—such as with the "þ"—an alternative letter with a diacritic, in this case the "t̄", is permitted. Only one of the current letters, the "q", is being dropped.

As a result of this, each sound is now spelled with exactly one letter, and each letter spells exactly one sound.

CONCLUSIONS

The issue of how a spoken language should be written is a very important one. After all, the ability to permanently record events and ideas is probably one of the greatest inventions in the entire history of humanity. Indeed, we know so much about the history of humanity precisely because of this invention. Likewise, before the invention of the telephone, writing allowed communication between people who were not standing next to one another.

Since the choice of writing system often involves issues of cultural heritage, including religion, it can often become emotional. Indeed, such considerations often take precedence over issues such as practicality.

As recent history has shown, spelling reforms can prove to be surprisingly controversial. In one sense, this is not entirely surprising given that, as was just mentioned, issues of cultural heritage are connected to the manner in which a given language is written. However, while the choice of writing system itself can clearly be a form of cultural heritage, along with even issues of which diacritics (if any) to use, updating the same system so as to make it more accurate need not be seen as a threat to cultural heritage. This is especially true if the writing system in question is designed to indicate the manner in which the words are to be pronounced. In such instances, the writing is merely a reflection of the manner in which the language in question is spoken.

If reforming the writing system is a threat to cultural heritage, then society should have been more adamant that the spoken language not change. Indeed, one could say that opposition to reforming the spelling system after pronunciation has changed is tantamount to killing the messenger. It should therefore be seen as no threat at all to a society's cultural heritage to update the writing system to take note of a society's change in pronunciation, especially if the same writing system is merely being updated and there is therefore no change in the writing system involved.

However, we must never lose sight of the fact that, while cultural heritage and even aesthetic beauty—after all, writing can be a beautiful form of art in its own right—are important, the main purpose of writing is for the want of communication. Communication itself is a neutral concept. As a result, a writing system needs to be practical. Indeed, probably the stupidest argument against spelling reform is that it dumbs down society. One of the ways in which societies advance is by making needlessly complicated systems easier.

Moreover, an alphabetic writing system—probably the world's most common—is designed to accurately reflect the manner in which words are spoken. The spoken language, however, often changes with time. If the spoken language changes, then so should the written language, at least in the case of writing systems that are designed to indicate the manner in which words are to be pronounced. This is especially true of alphabetic writing systems.

If ever there were a language using an alphabetic writing system in desperate need of reform, it is modern day English. In fact, the use of the word "modern" in this context is perhaps not fully accurate, as the need for spelling reform in English is not new. This study used numerous examples to show just how wildly unpredictable English spelling is. As this study mentioned, there were calls for spelling reform in English centuries ago. One could easily say that English orthography is basically just a rough guide that hints at how to pronounce the words in spoken English.

A quick search of spelling reforms in other languages will show that many of the other European languages that use the Latin alphabet have undergone some form of spelling reform in the past thirty years. Indeed, at least amongst the Western European languages, it would appear as if the majority have undergone some form of reform of orthography. That being the case, it seems strange that English—which needs spelling reform the most—is one of those that have not undergone any reform.

Part of the problem with reforming English orthography is that it is so bad with regards to the accuracy of phonetics to begin with, that the overall percentage of words that would have to change would be quite high, well above the other Western European languages which have recently had reforms. Indeed, depending on the specific details of the reform, it could easily be well over half of the words that will end up with a new spelling. One needs to only look at the appendix at the end of this study to see that well over 90% of the words now have a new spelling. However, there is an advantage to that as well: it allows English to make a clean break from the old system and thereby make a huge distinction with the new system. It would therefore lead to less mixing of the two systems, not that some mixing would be entirely a bad thing.

One other huge advantage: the reformed words are generally shorter. In fact, in the appendix, the 783 words in the current orthography are 3238 characters longer, whereas they are only 2774 characters in the reformed system with diacritics. Even without diacritics, they are slightly shorter, at 3216 characters.

As for the actual reform of English, the initial question is: should the current system start as a basis, or should the orthographic system start over anew? Also, should diacritics be used? The answer to the first question is that while the current orthographic system should be used as a starting point, it is more important that each sound has exactly one spelling and that each spelling makes exactly one sound.

As for diacritics, it is surprising how rare they are in English when compared to other European languages using the Latin alphabet, when one considers that English has more sounds than the other ones. Based on that fact, diacritics should certainly be used. This is especially true if the goal is to have a single letter for each sound: the Latin alphabet simply does not have enough letters in and of itself to spell the sounds of English with a different, single letter. However, since English speakers are not accustomed to diacritics, and it may be a bit more cumbersome writing on computers and cellphones with diacritics, an alternative system with no diacritics should be offered as well. After all, Swedish has a fixed, two-letter combination for each of the three diacritics in that language.

Related to the diacritic issue is the issue of whether to revive letters that once existed in English, but no longer do. This study concluded that some of these letters should be revived, but not others. This decision was based purely on practical considerations, as some of the letters would be useful, whereas others would not be. It is worth noting that if one of the concerns about spelling reform is that it threatens a society's cultural heritage, then what better way to assuage such concerns than to call upon the language's historical heritage?

There is no need to repeat the sound to letter suggestions that were made in the final chapter of this research. Likewise, it is also not necessary to repeat all of the practical issues associated with spelling reform. It is clear that the benefits outweigh any of the possible difficulties.

One final note though, no spelling reform would be better than a bad reform. Indeed, probably part of the reason that the recent French and German spelling reforms saw opposition may have been due more to the actual proposed reforms themselves, rather than the concept of spelling reform in general. Indeed, those particular reforms did not seem all that great. Therefore, opposition to them does not mean opposition to spelling reform in and of itself. In the end, no spelling reform in English would be better than a lousy reform.

Having stated all of that:

Let's fīnulē cāj ðu wā wē spel Iŋliš wurdz sō ðat it wil bē mor funetik!

REFERENCES

Accredited Language Services. (2019). Retrieved April 23, 2019 from https://www.alsintl.com/resources/languages/Creole/.

BBC. (2001). Education. Retrieved May 23, 2019 from http://news.bbc.co.uk/2/hi/uk_news/education/1225119.stm.

British Library. (2019). Language & Literature. Retrieved May 30, 2019 from http://www.bl.uk/learning/langlit/sounds/changing-voices/phonological-change/.

English Club. (2019). History of the English Language. Retrieved March 6, 2019 from https://www.englishclub.com/history-of-english/.

ESL Charts. (2019). Vowel Sound Charts. Retrieved April 23, 2019 from English http://www.eslcharts.com/english-vowel-sounds-chart.html.

Harvard. (2019). The Geoffrey Chaucer Page. Retrieved June 1, 2019 from http://sites.fas.harvard.edu/~chaucer/vowels.html.

Norwegian on the Web. (2019). Retrieved May 15, 2019 from https://www.ntnu.edu/now/intro/background-norwegian.

Omniglot. (2019). Retrieved May 1, 2019 from http://www.omniglot.com/writing/romanian.htm.

Omniglot. (2019). Benjamin Franklin's Phonetic Alphabet. Retrieved March 30, 2019 from http://www.omniglot.com/writing/franklin.htm.

Study English Today. (2019). A Brief History of English. Retrieved May 21, 2019 from http://www.studyenglishtoday.net/english-language-history.html.

The History of English. (2019). Great Vowel Shift. Retrieved May 1, 2019 from https://www.thehistoryofenglish.com/history_early_modern.html.

Språkrådet. (2019). Retrieved June 1, 2019 from https://www.sprakradet.no/Vi-og-vart/Om-oss/English-and-other-languages/English/norwegian-bokmal-vs.-nynorsk/.

Berlitz. (1985). *European Phrase Book.* Oxford: Berlitz Publishing Company.

Calvin, T. (1902). The Amelioration of Our Spelling. *PMLA, 17*(3), 297-311.

Coffey, N. (2017). *French Linguistics.* The French Spelling Reform. Retrieved April 28, 2019 from http://french-linguistics.co.uk/grammar/french_spelling_reform.shtml

Dawson, L. D. (1997). *Dicho y Hecho.* New York: John Wiley & Sons.

Dittrich, M. (2019). *Goethe Institut.* German Spelling Reform. Retrieved June 1, 2019 from https://www.goethe.de/en/spr/mag/20802137.html.

Donaldson, B. (1996). *Colloquial Dutch.* New York: Routledge.

Gruber, B. (2019). *Reader's Digest.* There Used to Be Six More Letters in the English Alphabet! Retrieved April 28, 2019 from: https://www.rd.com/culture/there-were-six-more-letters-in-our-alphabet/.

Harbeck, J. (2015, June 08). *BBC.* How the English Language Became such a Mess. Retrieved May 17, 2019 from http://www.bbc.com/culture/story/20150605-your-language-is-sinful

Hawkesworth, C. (1998). *Colloquial Croatian and Serbian.* London: Routledge.

Holy Bible (2011). The New Testament. Colorado Springs, CO: Biblica, Inc.

Johannes C. Ziegler, C. P.-W.-K. (2003). Developmental dyslexia in different languages: Language-specific or universal? *Experimental Child Psychology, 86*, 169-193.

Jones, P. A. (2016, November 3). *Mental Floss.* When Theodore Roosevelt Tried to Reform the English Language. Retrieved April 15, 2019 from http://mentalfloss.com/article/87691/when-theodore-roosevelt-tried-reform-english-language.

Jorgensen, J. H. (2000, January 26). *Department of Linguistics Brigham Young University.* History of the Georgian Language. Retrieved from May 13, 2019 http://linguistics.byu.edu/classes/Ling450ch/reports/Georgian1.html.

King, G. (1995). *Colloquial Welsh: A Complete Language Course.* London: Routledge.

Klein, K. (1964). Recent Soviet Discussion on Reform of Russian Orthography. *The Slavic and East European Journal, 8*(1).

Lancashire, A. (2015, May 14). *Euronews.* Portuguese language reform law goes global. Retrieved May 12, 2019 from https://www.euronews.com/2015/05/14/portuguese-language-reform-law-goes-global.

Lewis, G. (1999). *The Turkish Language Reform: a Catastrophic Success.* Oxford: Oxford University Press.

Marlowe, L. (2016, February 10). *The Irish Times.* French language reform becomes a cause célèbre. Retrieved May 10, 2019 from https://www.irishtimes.com/news/world/europe/french-language-reform-becomes-a-cause-célèbre-1.2528683.

Matsukas, A. (1997). *Teach Yourself Greek: A Complete Course For Beginners.* London: Hodder Headline Plc.

Poindexter, H. (2017, February 25). *We used to have six more letters in the English alphabet* Quartz. Retrieved March 13, 2019 from https://qz.com/914372/we-used-to-have-six-more-letters-in-the-english-alphabet/.

Powell, L. (1880). Spelling Reform. *National Journal of Education, 12*(2), 23.

Reuters. (2017, October 26). Alphabet soup as Kazakh leader orders switch from Cyrillic to Latin letters. *The Guardian.*

Robinson, A. (2007). *The Story of Writing.* London: Thames & Hudson.

Shakespeare, W. (1968). *Othello.* London: Penguin.

Sokolskaya, E. (2013, October 10). *Russian Life.* Spelling Reform: Who Gets the Credit? Retrieved April 15, 2019 from https://russianlife.com/stories/online/spelling-reform/.

Superville, D. (2006, July 5). Push for Simpler Spelling Persists. *The Washington Post.*

Watts, N. (2004). *Colloquial Greek.* London: Routledge.

Whitney. (1876). Spelling Reform. *New England Journal of Education, 4*(5), 55.

Zazulak, S. (2016, June 30). *Pearson.* 11 new English words – and how to use them. Retrieved April 20, 2019 from https://www.english.com/blog/new-english-words/.

Zimmer, B. (2010, June 25). Ghoti. *New York Times.*

APPENDIX 1: John- Chapter 3 (Holy Bible, New International Version) in the Current Orthography

1 Now there was a Pharisee, a man named Nicodemus who was a member of the Jewish ruling council.

2 He came to Jesus at night and said, "Rabbi, we know that you are a teacher who has come from God. For no one could perform the signs you are doing if God were not with him."

3 Jesus replied, "Very truly I tell you, no one can see the kingdom of God unless they are born again."

4 "How can someone be born when they are old?" Nicodemus asked. "Surely they cannot enter a second time into their mother's womb to be born!"

5 Jesus answered, "Very truly I tell you, no one can enter the kingdom of God unless they are born of water and the Spirit.

6 Flesh gives birth to flesh, but the Spirit gives birth to spirit.

7 You should not be surprised at my saying, 'You must be born again.'

8 The wind blows wherever it pleases. You hear its sound, but you cannot tell where it comes from or where it is going. So it is with everyone born of the Spirit."

9 "How can this be?" Nicodemus asked.

10 "You are Israel's teacher," said Jesus, "and do you not understand these things?

11 Very truly I tell you, we speak of what we know, and we testify to what we have seen, but still you people do not accept our testimony.

12 I have spoken to you of earthly things and you do not believe; how then will you believe if I speak of heavenly things?

13 No one has ever gone into heaven except the one who came from heaven—the Son of Man.

14 Just as Moses lifted up the snake in the wilderness, so the Son of Man must be lifted up,

15 that everyone who believes may have eternal life in him."

16 For God so loved the world that he gave his one and only Son, that whoever believes in him shall not perish but have eternal life.

17 For God did not send his Son into the world to condemn the world, but to save the world through him.

18 Whoever believes in him is not condemned, but whoever does not believe stands condemned already because they have not believed in the name of God's one and only Son.

19 This is the verdict: Light has come into the world, but people loved darkness instead of light because their deeds were evil.

20 Everyone who does evil hates the light, and will not come into the light for fear that their deeds will be exposed.

21 But whoever lives by the truth comes into the light, so that it may be seen plainly that what they have done has been done in the sight of God.

22 After this, Jesus and his disciples went out into the Judean countryside, where he spent some time with them, and baptized.

23 Now John also was baptizing at Aenon near Salim, because there was plenty of water, and people were coming and being baptized.

24 (This was before John was put in prison.)

25 An argument developed between some of John's disciples and a certain Jew over the matter of ceremonial washing.

26 They came to John and said to him, "Rabbi, that man who was with you on the other side of the Jordan—the one you testified about—look, he is baptizing, and everyone is going to him."

27 To this John replied, "A person can receive only what is given them from heaven.

28 You yourselves can testify that I said, 'I am not the Messiah but am sent ahead of him.'

29 The bride belongs to the bridegroom. The friend who attends the bridegroom waits and listens for him, and is full of joy when he hears the bridegroom's voice. That joy is mine, and it is now complete.

30 He must become greater; I must become less."

31 The one who comes from above is above all; the one who is from the earth belongs to the earth, and speaks as one from the earth. The one who comes from heaven is above all.

32 He testifies to what he has seen and heard, but no one accepts his testimony.

33 Whoever has accepted it has certified that God is truthful.

34 For the one whom God has sent speaks the words of God, for God gives the Spirit without limit.

35 The Father loves the Son and has placed everything in his hands.

36 Whoever believes in the Son has eternal life, but whoever rejects the Son will not see life, for God's wrath remains on them.

APPENDIX 2: John -Chapter 3 (Holy Bible, New International Version) in the Reformed Orthography with Diacritics

1 Nô ðer wuz u Ferusē, u man nāmd Nikodēmus hů wuz u membur uv ðu Jůiš růliŋ kônsul.

2 Hē kām tů Jēzus at nīt and sed, "Rabī, wē nō ðat ū ar u tēcur hů haz kum frum God. For nō wun kúd purform ðu sīnz ū ar důiŋ if God wur not wið him."

3 Jēzus riplīd, "Verē trůlē Ī tel ū, nō wun kan sē ðu kiŋdum uv God unles ðā ar born ugen."

4 "Hô kan sumwun bē born wen ðā ar ōld?" Nikodēmus askt. "Šurlē ðā kannot entur u sekund tīm intů ðer moður's wům tů bē born!"

5 Jēzus ansurd, "Verē trůlē Ī tel ū, nō wun kan entur ðu kiŋdum uv God unles ðā ar born uv watur and ðu Spirit.

6 Fleš givz burþ tů fleš, but ðu Spirit givz burþ tů spirit.

7 Ū šúd not bē surprīzd at mī sāiŋ, 'Ū must bē born ugen.'

8 Ðu wind blōz werevur it plēzez. Ū hir its sônd, but ū kannot tel wer it kumz frum or wer it iz gōiŋ. Sō it iz wið evrēwun born uv ðu Spirit."

9 "Hô kan ðis bē?" Nikodēmus askt.

10 "Ū ar Izrēul's tēcur," sed Jēzus, "and dů ū not undurstand ðēz þiŋz?

11 Verē trůlē Ī tel ū, wē spēk uv wut wē nō, and wē testifī tů wut wē hav sēn, but stil ū pēpul dů not aksept ôr testimōnē.

12 Ī hav spōken tů ū uv urþlē þiŋz and ū dů not belēv; hô ðen wil ū belēv if Ī spēk uv hevenlē þiŋz?

13 Nō wun haz evur gon intů heven exsept ðu wun hů kām frum heven—ðu Sun uv Man.

14 Just az Mōzes lifted up ðu snāk in ðu wildurnes, sō ðu Sun uv Man must bē lifted up,

15 ðat evrēwun hů belēvz mā hav ēturnal līf in him."

16 For God sō luvd ðu wurld ðat Hē gāv hiz wun and ōnlē Sun, ðat hůever belēvz in him šal not periš but hav ēturnal līf.

17 For God did not send hiz Sun intů ðu wurld tů kundem ðu wurld, but tů sāv ðu wurld þrů him.

18 Hůever belēvz in him iz not kundemed, but hůever duz not belēv standz kundemed alredē bēkuz ðā hav not belēvd in ðu nām uv God's wun and ōnlē Sun.

19 Ðis iz ðu vurdikt: Līt haz kum intů ðu wurld, but pēpul luvd darknes insted uv līt bēkuz ðer dēdz wur ēvul.

20 Evrēwun hů duz ēvul hāts ðu līt, and wil not kum intů ðu līt for fir ðat ðer dēdz wil bē expōzd.

21 But hůever livs bī ðu trůþ kumz intů ðu līt, sō ðat it mā bē sēn plānlē ðat wut ðā hav dun haz bin dun in ðu sīt uv God.

22 Aftur ðis, Jēzus and hiz disīpuls went ôt intů ðu Jūdean kuntrīsīd, wer Hē spent sum tīm wið ðem, and baptīzd.

23 Nô Jon alsō wuz baptīziŋ at Aenon nir Salim, bēkuz ðer wuz plentē uv watur, and pēpul wur kumiŋ and bēiŋ baptīzd.

24 (Ðis wuz bēfor Jon wuz pút in prizun.)

25 An argūment developt betwēn sum uv Jon's disīpuls and u surtun Jū over ðu matur uv serumōmēal wošiŋ.

26 Ðā kām tů Jon and sed tů him, "Rabī, ðat man hů wuz wið ū on ðu oður sīd uv ðu Jordun—ðu wun ū testifīd about—look, Hē iz baptīziŋ, and evrēwun iz gōiŋ tů him."

27 Tů ðis Jon riplīd, "U pursun kan risēv ōnlē wut iz given ðem frum heven.

28 Ū ūrselvz kan testifī ðat Ī sed, 'Ī am not ðu Musīu but am sent uhed uv him.'

29 Ðu brīd bēloŋz tů ðu brīdgrům. Ðu frend hů atendz ðu brīdgrům wāts and lisens for him, and iz ful uv jœ wen Hē hirs ðu brīdgrům's vœs. Ðat jœ iz mīn, and it iz nô kumplēt.

30 Hē must bēkum grātur; Ī must bēkum les."

31 Ðu wun hů kumz frum ubuv iz ubuv ol; ðu wun hů iz frum ðu urþ bēloŋz tů ðu urþ, and spēks az wun frum ðu urþ. Ðu wun hů kumz frum heven iz ubuv ol.

32 Hē testifīz tů wut Hē haz sēn and hurd, but nō wun aksepts hiz testimōnē.

33 Hůever haz aksepted it haz surtifīd ðat God iz trůþful.

34 For ðu wun hům God haz sent spēks ðu wurdz uv God, for God givz ðu Spirit wiðôt limit.

35 Ðu Faður luvs ðu Sun and haz plāst evrēþiŋ in hiz hands.

36 Hůever belēvz in ðu Sun haz ēturnal līf, but hůever rejekts ðu Sun wil not sē līf, for God's raþ remāns on ðem.

APPENDIX 3: John -Chapter 3 (Holy Bible, New International Version) in the Reformed Orthography without Diacritics

1 Now dher wuz u Ferusee, u man naymd Nikodeemus hoo wuz u membur uv dhu Jooish rooling kownsul.

2 Hee kaym too Jeezus at niit and sed, "Rabii, wee noa dhat yoo ar u teecur hoo haz kum frum God. For noa wun kuud purform dhu siinz yoo ar dooing if God wur not widh him."

3 Jeezus ripliid, "Veree troolee II tel yoo, noa wun kan see dhu kingdom uv God unles dhay ar born ugen."

4 "How kan sumwun bee born wen dhay ar oald?" Nikodeemus askt. "Shurlee dhay kannot entur u sekund tiim intoo dher modhur's woom too bee born!"

5 Jeezus ansurd, "Veree troolee II tel yoo, noa wun kan entur dhu kingdom uv God unles dhay ar born uv watur and dhu Spirit.

6 Flesh givz burth too flesh, but dhu Spirit givz burth too spirit.

7 YOO shuud not bee surpriizd at mii saying, 'YOO must bee born ugen.'

8 DHu wind bloaz werevur it pleezez. YOO hir its sownd, but yoo kannot tel wer it kumz frum or wer it iz goaing. Soa it iz widh evreewun born uv dhu Spirit."

9 "How kan dhis bee?" Nikodeemus askt.

10 "YOO ar Izreeul's teecur," sed Jeezus, "and doo yoo not undurstand dheez thingz?

11 Veree troolee II tel yoo, wee speek uv wut wee noa, and wee testifii too wut wee hav seen, but stil yoo peepul doo not aksept owr testimoanee.

12 II hav spoaken too yoo uv urthlee thingz and yoo doo not beleev; how dhen wil yoo beleev if II speek uv hevenlee thingz?

13 Noa wun haz evur gon intoo heven exsept dhu wun hoo kaym frum heven—dhu Sun uv Man.

14 Just az Moazes lifted up dhu snayk in dhu wildurnes, soa dhu Sun uv Man must bee lifted up,

15 dhat evreewun hoo beleevz may hav eeturnal liif in him."

16 For God soa luvd dhu wurld dhat Hee gayv hiz wun and oanlee Sun, dhat hooever beleevz in him shal not perish but hav eeturnal liif.

17 For God did not send hiz Sun intoo dhu wurld too kundem dhu wurld, but too sayv dhu wurld throo him.

18 Hooever beleevz in him iz not kundemed, but hooever duz not beleev standz kundemed alredee beekuz dhay hav not beleevd in dhu naym uv God's wun and oanlee Sun.

19 Dhis iz dhu vurdikt: Liit haz kum intoo dhu wurld, but peepul luvd darknes insted uv liit beekuz dher deedz wur eevul.

20 Evreewun hoo duz eevul hayts dhu liit, and wil not kum intoo dhu liit for fir dhat dher deedz wil bee expoazd.

21 But hooever livs bii dhu trooth kumz intoo dhu liit, soa dhat it may bee seen playnlee dhat wut dhay hav dun haz bin dun in dhu siit uv God.

22 Aftur dhis, Jeezus and hiz disiipuls went owt intoo dhu Jyoodean kuntriisiid, wer Hee spent sum tiim widh dhem, and baptiizd.

23 Now Jon alsoa wuz baptiizing at Aenon nir Salim, beekuz dher wuz plentee uv watur, and peepul wur kuming and beeing baptiizd.

24 (Dhis wuz beefor Jon wuz puut in prizun.)

25 An argyooment developt between sum uv Jon's disiipuls and u surtun Jyoo over dhu matur uv serumoameeal woshing.

26 Dhay kaym too Jon and sed too him, "Rabii, dhat man hoo wuz widh yoo on dhu odhur siid uv dhu Jordun—dhu wun yoo testifiid about—look, Hee iz baptiizing, and evreewun iz goaing too him."

27 Too dhis Jon ripliid, "U pursun kan riseev oanlee wut iz given dhem frum heven.

28 Yoo yoorselvz kan testifii dhat II sed, 'II am not dhu Musiiu but am sent uhed uv him.'

29 Dhu briid beelongz too dhu briidgroom. Dhu frend hoo atendz dhu briidgroom wayts and lisens for him, and iz ful uv joy wen Hee hirs dhu briidgroom's voys. Dhat joy iz miin, and it iz now kumpleet.

30 Hee must beekum graytur; II must beekum les."

31 Dhu wun hoo kumz frum ubuv iz ubuv ol; dhu wun hoo iz frum dhu urth beelongz too dhu urth, and speeks az wun frum dhu urth. Dhu wun hoo kumz frum heven iz ubuv ol.

32 Hee testifiiz too wut Hee haz seen and hurd, but noa wun aksepts hiz testimoanee.

33 Hooever haz aksepted it haz surtifiid dhat God iz troothful.

34 For dhu wun hoom God haz sent speeks dhu wurdz uv God, for God givz dhu Spirit widhowt limit.

35 Dhu Fadhur luvs dhu Sun and haz playst evreething in hiz hands.

36 Hooever beleevz in dhu Sun haz eeturnal liif, but hooever rejekts dhu Sun wil not see liif, for God's rath remayns on dhem.

ABOUT THE AUTHOR

Dr. Carl Augustsson was born in the United States in 1977 to a mother from the United States and a father from Sweden. His wife is from the Republic of Georgia. As a result, he has citizenship in all three countries and by extension, the European Union. He has four Master's degrees and a PhD in various Liberal Arts fields such as Political Science and English Philology. His favorite hobbies are world travel (He has been to over 100 countries) and studying languages (He has studied over two dozen languages in some capacity.) Carl is passionate about languages and writing systems.

www.ingramcontent.com/pod-product-compliance
Lightning Source LLC
LaVergne TN
LVHW051039070526
838201LV00066B/4859